The TRAP

(The Truth Revealed)

Andy Cooper

Prolific Purchasing Properties & Publications, LLC
LYNCHBURG, VIRGINIA

Prolific Purchasing Properties & Publications, LLC
prolificpublications@gmail.com

Publisher's Note: This is a work of non-fiction. Situations, places, and incidents are prod-ucts of the author's perceptions, perspectives & possession. Some details may have been reformed to protect identities; every effort has been made by the author to avoid specifi-cations & pin-pointing. Any resemblance to actual persons, living or dead, or to business-es, companies, events, institutions, organizations or locales is completely coincidental. While the author has made every effort to provide accurate Internet & mailing addresses at the time of publication, neither the publisher nor the author assumes any responsibility for errors or for changes that occur after publication. Unless otherwise noted, all Scrip-ture will be used from one of these versions of the Holy Bible: KJV, NKJV, NIV, The Message &/or ESV. BOOK COVER ART DISCLAIMER: The art for the book cover is a compilation of transformative elements structured to create a singular item of use. The original art pieces were NOT created by this author, NOR this publisher, but were creat-ed &/or ARE OWNED by the following: Original Owner of the "Bleeding Heart" art/graphic is Lily Jones lily@lilyvanilli.com [lilyvanilli.com]; Original Owner of the "Bear Trap" art/graphic is Volker Troy, affiliate of CGSociety [CGSociety.com]. Author's Photograph taken by S. Wright Photography ©

Internal Layout ©2017 BookDesignTemplates.com

Ordering Information:
Quantity sales. Special discounts are available on quantity purchases by corporations, associations, and others. For details, contact the "Special Sales Department" at the ad-dress above.

The TRAP (The Truth Revealed)/ Andy Cooper. -- 1st ed.
ISBN: 978-0-692-92571-3
ISBN: 0-692-92571-6
Library of Congress Control Number: 2017912880

THANK YOUS

- First of all:

  I MUST say thank You to GOD, the Great I AM, the Creator of All, the MASTER of the Universe, Yoshua (Jesus), the Almighty *Living* Truth & Power of God – MASTER of ALL EXISTENCE. Without You, O God, I *truly* am nothing. I recognize that I am mere dust.

  I do not understand why out of all people, You would allow ME to live. I do not understand why You would ever fight for me. – Why You would reveal secret, deceptive Truths to me about people for *my* protection... --Why You would forgive someone like me, who blatantly has chosen, time & time again to disobey You due to selfishness, fear & doubt? I know the Power of Yoshua's (Jesus') Blood is REAL & that it covers sin, because it is I... who still has breath in her body! Your Blood is the RECONCILER!!! I know that Your Holy Spirit is Alive & Almighty.

I am EVER grateful that You would *ever* consider using me for *any*thing good. The only Good that I am, IS...You, Lord King. And I hope to make You proud, *not just with this book*, but with my Life & my Living. I love You, Lord Jesus. And I thank You!

- To my Pastors: Apostle Kelso & Apostle Jacqueline Clark...
  –truly God is alive and well. I know this because of You. I know that God IS Love because of You. I *now* know that Love is *real* because of you. When I did not

know HOW to Love...your ACTIONS taught me how. I am a witness to the Power of the Holy Spirit because of you. I know that a life of holiness *can* render favor & blessings because of you. I know that prayers work & miracles **can** manifest through *our own* obedience, declaration & faith because of you. I know how to truly praise & worship God **with my spirit** because of what you've taught & <u>lived</u>. If it wasn't for your acceptance of God's call upon your lives I'd be dead, in jail or in an asylum, assuredly.

You believed in me when *everyone* else gave up on me, **including** myself. *To do the things you've done for God's ministry & God's people*: the sacrificial Living, the prayers, the fasting, the financial sowing, *being* steadfast, good stewards...it's mind-blowing! I do not understand why God would have *allowed me* to be connected to you. (Smh)

I know Jesus' Blood is real because it has prevented me from dropping dead in God's Presence (your office–*Hello!*). You've **inspired** faith in me. You've **resuscitated** my spirit, the *many* times that I was 'down for the count' & the enemy, the devil was slapping the spiritual-mat beside my spiritual-head.

Truthfully, there were countless times & even *years*...

that I thought that you didn't care about my feelings. But I now realize that you were only training & raising me to be a **STRONG** warrior in God. –That feelings *cannot* be considered when obeying God & that often times, feelings is how we get 'tricked' *out* of the blessing.

I am forever indebted to God in you, Apostle Kelso & Apostle Jacqueline Clark. I pray that no matter where God leads you or *me*, that I will always be a close-knit part of your hearts & your lives.

- To my mother, Pamela Wright Garrett:
  I thank you for all that you *sacrificed* to make sure that I was taken care of. I finally understand that you yourself have been hurt so much & overly unconsidered that it created great pain that traveled with you the majority, if not all of your life. I know now, that no matter what hurt I may have experienced in any time spent with you, that you loved me with your entire heart.

  I stand proxy, <u>for all individuals</u> that neglected you, abused or misused you, under-appreciated you, forgot you, stole from you, lied on you & lied to you, left you &/or hurt you: by saying "*I am sorry. I apologize. I was wrong.*"

You need to know, Momma, that you are a beautiful person. Not just your spirit & your mind; you are physically beautiful as well. There aren't many women who choose to *not* wear makeup or nail polish & can *still be* noticeably attractive. But *you* are.

I am sorry that no one ever told you appropriately that you are good-looking & that no one took the time to invest in your self-esteem. You are wise. You are thorough. You are strong. You are funny. You are SU-PER-intelligent. You...are an asset.

I pray that God will help you take the limitations off of your own heart & your own mind & that you will seek & strive to achieve the things in life that you *always wanted* to have. (You CAN still be a pharmacist.) With God, all things are possible.

Thank you for your prayers. <u>And thank you for **still** loving me, when the hours of contradiction **tried** to make you think I would *never* love you.</u> KNOW Momma: that I <u>can</u> *finally* say, "I do love you" and mean it with *all* sincerity. And again...I thank you for loving me, through 'it' all.

- To my sister, Alicia Noelle Garrett:
  I don't think that you'll ever really understand the

love that I have for you. There are so many things that I tried to protect you from. And like most children, you went & sought those very things...

It is through faith that I now I have to release you into God's Hands of Protection. I speak the Word over your Life. I declare that only God's Will, will be done in your Life.

You will not walk in, not operate in, & not manifest any generational curse. <u>I decree that God has even now, endowed you with *supernatural* wisdom & discernment so that you will always know when the enemy is trying to deceive you, trap you & ruin your spirit, heart & Life.</u> I decree that you will not get pregnant out of wedlock & you will only marry the man that God has *preordained* for your Life, before God ever said "Let there be light..."

You are multi-talented & gifted: an artist, a poet/author, a jeweler, fashion designer, a singer, an actor, a sculptor...these gifts MUST NOT go to waste, Alicia. <u>Anyone in your life that is not trying to promote these gifts positively & direct you on a path to success</u> (in these areas) <u>is an assassin to your destiny & they</u>

<u>only seek to use you & deceive you</u>. This in-
cludes...*yourself.*

Do not think or behave like a child. <u>Do nottttttt trust
in people's words</u>!!! Choose to trust & pray to God &
<u>HE</u> WILL *protect* you, *lead* you, & *guide* you in the
ways that you *should* go & <u>He will</u> tell you what people
you should & should not believe in; GUARANTEED!
(John 16:13)
God will expose ALL *counterfeits* and *wolves* (male &
female) when you seek Him for the answers.

No one has loved me like you. And I am grateful to
know at the end of every day, that you are my 'cheer-
leader', my friend, she –who will cry with me & is concerned about me. And I pray that we will get closer &
closer through time. If you ever need *Sissy*, let me
know...

- To my cousin Sam:
  –My first friend. You are included in every memory.
  You've been there since the beginning, being only 1
  year younger than me. I have loved you so much. We
  were raised as sisters...again, my first friend.
  I want to tell you that I am sorry for the hurts that
  you've experienced in your Life. I know that *emotionally* you are tough due to past circumstances & like

me; some would *consider* you hard to love. But, you ARE loveable & like Alicia, you are multi-talented. You should be getting paid for your gifts & I pray that you will have enough faith one day to believe that Jesus *intentionally* gave you these gifts (photography, hair, nails, financial management) so that you can have many streams of income.

I want to apologize to you & your family (the Wright-Blakes) for being an **improper** example of how one *should* live for Christ.

There were many times that you saw me say & do things that are not Christ-like. I did not & do not want you to think that these things were/are acceptable. Selfishly, I 'ran' to your home, when I wanted to 'get away' from the *expectations of the Life in God*. Please know that my chosen weaknesses do not take away from God's Power or the Power that can be released into one's Life when *truly* doing God's Word & Living His Way.

I pray that you & I will find a way to be more selfless, that we will be alive & always in communication until Jesus returns. No! <u>You do NOT have to die!</u> (The Word says that we shall not all 'sleep'; *Google*, if necessary, to locate it.)

Andy Cooper

→I pray that God will manifest immediately the perfect situation that is needed to destroy your doubts about His Word & His Existence & birth (in you) TRUE, unshakeable faith *in Him*, just like He did in *me*; –the former cynical one.
I love you, Sammie.

- To all my aunts, uncles & cousins:
  I know you guys love me! You guys are just like me! We always say, *'we are nice people, but don't you cross us!'* (LOL!) There is nothing better than to be **understood** and cared for & cared about.
  Truly you all make me feel cared about. *It doesn't matter the length of time we haven't seen each other*, we always greet each other with a hug & a kiss & depart the same way. Nothing can compare to that! This world is SO cold & FAKE-hearted in every venue in Life. And when I've felt empty & alone, I've managed to *eventually* find myself in your company & walked away feeling like, somehow, everything will be alright.

Thanking for loving me: *Grandmother* (actually my great-grandmother: Margreed Brown Withers) & *Mother* (actually my grandmother: Dallie Ann(ie) Wright–I wish you could have known how much I Loved you, *Mother*), Aunt Karen (I'm sorry that I didn't understand & I miss you), Uncle Winston, Aunt

Sheila (2 of a loving-kind, down to earth), Uncle Doug & Aunt Loretta (2 angels in the earth), Aunt Melinda (I love you), Uncle John (I love you), Aunt Jenny (sing on!), Uncle Joe (you *know* I'm the winner! ☺), **Uncle Mark** (u get your own 'shot-out'), my step-father, Douglas Michael Garrett (thank you for stepping in; it's unfortunate that you didn't realize your worth); my cousins: DiAnna (& Willie, both always so nice), Micheal (still love you, Mikey---just like my brother, not my cousin), Devonn (quit being so mean! LOL), Darius (still acting like somebody's daddy), LaTasha (you are so beautiful; realize your value), Lore'l (Damien; Congratulations to you both), Brian (my little bro: B-D-Bs), Briana (my little sis: GO TO SCHOOL, Bri!), Alex (looking like his mama), Reese (e-cup), Sam (pop), Wise (off the hook smart), Lazarus (you have the most gorgeous smile, you made me genuinely smile even when my heart was breaking with tears running down my face) & the precious & special Livia, & to DiAnna's unborn (find out what on 9-15-13; _now_ *Born*: William George Palmer) & little Nevajah-looking like her daddy's twin; (& Micheal's babies; & Brian's babies) I love you all FOREVER!!!

- To Regina Tweedy:
  A lady (a southern belle) in a cold & evil world. A rare breed. So *particular* in your ways. (I've never met any-

one that was hungry and would <u>not</u> eat standing up! The *lady* in you prefers hunger if a table, a plate & cutlery isn't involved! Smh...) *I'll stand on one leg, eating a bag of chips if necessary* (LOL)!

The one thing that I <u>do</u> know about *me*, is that if someone likes me, then they not only like me, but they *actually* love me, *even* if they don't admit it. I am not an easy person to befriend. If someone chooses to be friends with me, *it's because they appreciate* what I STAND for & what I BELIEVE in. I am <u>not</u> the friend that calls all the time, nor the one that will hang out often. I tell only the info that I feel comfortable telling & sometimes I can be very aloof. **Despite this**, you love me. Despite this, you care. Despite this, you appreciate me. Despite this, you pray for me. Despite this, you cry *with* & *for* me. Despite this, you encourage me when I want to give up. Despite this, you forgive me when I am rude & rigid. You've rubbed my back when internally, I was secretly-suffering & screaming-silently.

I am praying with & for you concerning the things that you are believing God for. God WILL NOT FORGET YOUR LABOR(s) of LOVE!

You indirectly taught me how to be soft in my *heart*.

And every time my heart tried to 'ice' over, your meekness made me melt and apologize. Your consistent actions created a special place in my heart for you...I thank you for all that you've said, did & do.

- To Sonja Punch:
or should I say Son-jaa! (Ha!) Always re-creating yourself...& I am not mad at you! *'Dare to be different'*, is what I believe. (There will ALWAYS be SOMEbody that will try to copy you & try to 'BE' you (low-key)-SMH!; so you <u>got</u> to switch it up *sometimes*; <u>**trust me**</u>, I know!!!)

You are my first client, in *image consulting*. I am so <u>mad</u> that I didn't take *'Before'* pictures of you!!! We might have to go buy some of those old church outfits, so we can have a 'Before & After' shot for my portfolio! No one would believe it unless they saw it!

You are the one that has truly operated <u>in</u>, <u>through</u>, & <u>by</u> the Holy Spirit & saw PAST *any* façade that I tried to display. *Spiritually*, you saw past my "beauty pageant smile" (...as *you've* termed) & saw the pain hiding in my heart.

Like Regina, you've loved me in spite of my distance. You cared for me, when I didn't call. Regardless of time, we always picked back up, as if no time had passed. My 'conference roll-dog': You were mature enough & loving enough & humble enough to (eventually) work with me through any disagreements we've ever had. For these things, I know you love me, in your own way, *somehow.*

God didn't give you the gift of singing & the desire to do so for no reason. Opportunity is coming, so be prepared. "Preparation brings peace" (Personal quote, given to me, by God). So...Get ready.
I can't wait to meet your husband; who will be militant like you! (LOLLLLLL!) But you will get to see the sweet side of him & this is the way that it should be.
I can't wait to see you walking the red carpet in California. They haven't *seen style* till I dress you! I believe in you. Don't stop believing in your (TRUE) self.

- To Tina Clark:
  Ms. Lady-Jewel. The girlie-girl who makes it ok to be overly feminine, *sometimesssss* (LOL!). With the 'tee-hees' and all! We've been through a lot. You alone have been through a lot. It is SUCH a blessing to see you move on in your career half way across the country, after bumming rides to work & school ALL those years ago! Watching your life has really motivated faith in me. Girl! You are ANOINTED to get a job, man! I'm so glad you broke free from those people who didn't appreciate you.

I pray that all your dreams come true. And I don't doubt they will.

Do not give your haters a second thought (the haters that are self-proclaimed & the haters that are chameleons, <u>always</u> staring, yet hiding)! God will continue to repay your haters, by *blessing <u>you</u>*. Just continue to bless God's Name & serve Him, OBEY Him & Live for Him <u>*only*</u>.

Your son will be known world-wide. He has success all over him & has *since* being a child. I am grateful for those days I spent at your home chillin' with Buddy (Lil' Andrés), your brothers Josh & Joseph Dews (now my brothers) & your mom, Carol Clark, the <u>BEST</u> chicken & fish fryer God created! (I really hope that Carol will get her *Bed & Breakfast* one day!) You guys made me a part of your family & I am appreciative!

I will always remember our NUMEROUS talks into early dawn. For some reason, God chose to connect us spiritually. I am grateful for you loving me. My 'hardness' & your 'softness' was <u>such</u> a contradiction! But I realize now, that God used us to balance *each other* out; you helped me be more malleable & I helped you to develop a 'thicker skin'. I hope that we can be close a Life-time through. And I have a strong feeling that we always will.

- To Miss Selena Austin:

  My HERO! There are <u>NOTTTTT</u> a lot of people that
  I admire, Selena. Really... I cannot use all the fingers
  on ONE of my hands to count the number! But, I do
  admire you.

  WHY? Because you are smart, sensible, beautiful,
  <u>non-fake</u>, wise <u>& you are not a **PUNKKKKKKK**</u>!!!
  Your HEART is true & genuine & your motives *towards **me*** (& countless others) are pure like water!

  So many people cower down to clicks & peer pressure
  <u>(even in church & ministries)</u>, for fear of ostracism,
  but not you! If it's *wrong*, it's *wrong* & you have <u>**no**</u>
  problem saying so. You don't let people pressure you
  into **ANY**thing.

  And if _***you***_ are wrong, you have NO problem apologiz-
  ing! I have learned that there are
  VERYYYYYYYYYYY few people who will sincerely
  apologize for simple things, & **even <u>fewer</u> people** who
  will apologize for BIG things, _*even in the house of*_
  God. **<u>But not you</u>**; you are <u>very</u> meek & mild. This is to
  be celebrated! This is why I am mentioning it now.

And it's so funny, because you are *so* humble that I know you are shocked & surprised that I would include you in my *Thank Yous*. But that's HOW much of an impact you've made in my Life. I've learned you must acknowledge the people in your Life that have made a remarkable difference. Your humility teaches me. Your quiet servitude unto God & our Apostles is a *proper* example. Your courage in your business venture is: admirable, exceptional & is...'BRILLIANCE REVEALED'!!!

Continue as you have, *refusing* to settle for less, in your own life & in ministry. God's going to take you up high, Selena! Yes, you will be married & he will be loving & <u>faithful</u> to you. And don't worry about Sequan. God has him all taken care of. Just continue to be the skilled director of his Life that you are.

I love you. Thank you for <u>ALL</u> your words of encouragement, at the times where I *least* expected, yet *needed* it the MOST! (FOR REAL, Selena...You were continually led by The Holy Spirit...every...single...time. Never let ANYone tell you that you do not hear from Yahweh God!)

- To Valerie Rose:
  Pastor Val! Smh. There is TOO much that could be

said when it comes to thanking you. You were the mighty, spiritual warrior, who <u>never</u> left her spiritual post. When I was out of spiritual-order & you were left alone with duties/assignments (& the like), & you stood **strong, unwavering**, even when all hell was breaking loose around you. I've learned **so much** from you through the years. And I'm grateful for our <u>new</u> understanding of each other.

You are the iron that God is using to sharpen my iron. I've learned with you, through God –that *<u>if two people are willing to truthfully put aside all preconceived notions that each held about the other person previously</u>*, then a NEW, *fresh* relationship can be had & **that** relationship can be genuine!!!

You are a smart, super-caring, extremely-organized, insightful, faithful, funny, fervent woman of God. It's my prayer that God will bless you & your husband for the thousands of hours & days & years that you've served God without complaint. You are an example to innumerable multitudes. You are a treasure & your gifts are all needed in God's Kingdom. Continue to walk for Jesus (confidently).

- Mother Barbara Booty:
  I tell you what...You are a *feisty*-one! And so full of

God that it doesn't make any sense! I don't even *know* when I fell in love with you, Mother Barbara. I guess it was when I realized that you were not *fake*.

You love The Lord Jesus & haven't *(shown me)* that you tried to be perfect. Yet you've grown & progressed higher in your *own* spiritual Life...and to see that growth is encouraging to me! Sometimes we get discouraged because we believe that we should have accomplished a certain amount of things in a certain amount of time. But you've shown me (directly & indirectly through *your* Life) that later is better than never. God still honors the heart & the True effort of His people.

You are a praying woman of God. And you've prayed my soul & spirit out of hell many times! You let me be as raw *as I could be* around you (when I started loosing religion, for **real**–*Hallelujah*!) & you didn't waver OR flinch at the rawness. You spiritually 'dug in' with me; and **now** look...once again, Yahweh God has answered your prayers. I thank you so much for loving me when very few people *could* or even knew *how* to.

- To Larry & Juanita Jefferson:
  Shaking my dag-gone head. There is absolutely TOO much that I want to say to the two of you. But I had to

mention your names because *when no one else would even speak to me OR even LOOK at me*...you SOUGHT me; you chased me down JUST...to hug me. You ran after me just to say, "*Don't give up. I love you. And God loves you too.*" Just typing this is bringing tears to my eyes.

When I thought that I'd given up on '*church*' & it's '*processes*'...your Christ-Love found a Way to penetrate the stone that I'd *become*. Others saw me as rebellious–'help'. But you saw me as a tried–'soul'. And *every time* you came after me, when I tried to make a 'quick get-a-way', you sowed the seeds of Love & Hope into my heart.

Now, as I type this & cry, please know that I will <u>never</u> forget this TRUE labor of spiritual Love. A lot of people 'talk' it in God's Kingdom & in God's Church. But when it comes to bleakness, very few can do what the two of you (spiritually) do...*naturally*. Forever I thank you. And please know that I will *never*... forget...

• To Uncle Mark (a.k.a: Pop):
Who is as amazing as you are? Who is as spiritually strong as you are? Whose spirit is as attractive as yours? Who is as financially frugal & sensible? Who is as caring? Who is as wise as you? Who is as well-

balanced? There is no one that I know or *heard* of who is as nice as you... that is so spiritually attractive that strangers automatically become lifetime-friends (literally).

You've opened my eyes, mind & heart to the possibility that one can **truly** live a life of Dreams & High Expectations through Diligence & Wise decisions. *The* *absolute best day of my life* (so far) *was spent intimately alone with you,* LITERALLY *in the middle of the sea,* 20 miles from Venezuela's borders –in that infinity pool in Curacao, leaning over the edge, talking about Life, while looking at the sea & the crabs crawling on the rocks below.

–To the man who saw his first ballet in Moscow (while some people living will **never** see a ballet, **nor** go to Russia!): If there is anyone that I would want to make proud, it is you. There have been times, that I would be around you, when I was *so sad* & I just didn't have the words or the heart to share the obscurity...that simply being in your presence made me feel better!

Even now, as you are working conscientiously WITH God to be restored physically back to your former self after your heart attack 2½ years ago (at the time of writing; now 6 years near publishing); I've seen really how strong you are (mentally, emotionally, physically, socially & spiritually). I cannot honestly say that I would be as loving, meek, mild, encouraged, positive & as *focused* as you are, laying in a bed for all these years, believing that you WILL WALK AGAIN, as you did *once* before. (AND YOU WILL unquestionably WALK AGAIN, POP!!!)

But even still! God has blessed my Life with *allowing* me to see you now being able to drive your own mechanical wheelchair (knocking over Stove-Top© Stuffing stands in Walmart; LOL!), to move your hands while you talk, to tell me your feet are tingling! Some people NEVER again, experience these things after the spinal cord injury that you encountered. Yet, here again, God is using YOU as HIS testimony of HIS Power, to defy ALL odds & defy ALL expectations!

To the world-traveler that had compassion on me and decided that I would be the one that he would share his *Life*, his *thoughts*, his *tactics* & his *secrets* to: I am grateful, forever so grateful for your Love & your consideration of me. You have been there for me SO MUCH–all of my Life, time & time again. Even when I was doing wrong & you let me go my *own* way, like a true father, you waited for me to realize the Truth &

return. And when I did return, you accepted me &
loved me.

You built me up. You explained my tears. You mur-
dered my fears. You exposed my Life to networking.
**You showed me the world is accessible _TO_ ME & that <u>I</u>
<u>do NOT have to settle</u> for the mediocre desires, medio-
cre hopes & mediocre plans that most people around
me possess & accept for** _themselves!_

_You taught me that it is okay for me to be the <u>only</u> one
that thinks <u>differently</u>._ From you, I learned that I
CAN be separate; I CAN be unusual; I CAN be successful. And all of this is _ok._

Like with all others that I love, I pray that you will
forever be alive & WELL, IN my Life, _right_ up until
the moment that Jesus cracks that huge sky with His
Physical Presence. I want to **always** be close to you
emotionally & mentally. I want my children to call you
Grandpop.

I need you; and I am so thankful that it is YOU who
<u>**never**</u> mistreats my vulnerability, like so many other
people (male & female –who claimed they care about
me) _have done._ I love you forever. I pray that God will

bless me extensively, so I can be that same blessing to you.

- To Terri Payne:
  Oh my GOSHHHH!!!
  How in the world am I supposed to sum up how I feel about you, '*Clack*', a.k.a. '*Thundah*'? LOLLLLLLL. Even if the amount of words that you <u>actually</u> see written in this 'thank you' TO you is few, that does not by ANY means indicate what you are & what you *mean* to me.

  As you know, I am not an easily, impressed person. But I can say that *you* impress me. Foremost, *it's your honest spirit & nature that impresses me.* Secondly, would be how thorough & true you are. You do not 'shuck & jive', 'beat around the bush', or 'tip-toe through the tulips', as they say! If I ever have a question to where I did not understand why you did or said something, *you <u>never</u> make me* 'work' to get the Truth...**you just give Truth** (whether negative or positive), because that's what you **are**...Truth.

  You have been such an inspiration for me to want to *do* & *be* better. You have overcome so MANY adversities in your own personal life. As you already know, it's only by God's Grace that you made the accomplishments that you have & become the beautiful person (inside & out) that you are.

You know me; and I'm all about that real. I don't like wasting my time on people or things that aren't. And even though I sensed **instantly** that you were real when I first met you; you PROVED it to me that time when we were in the Dominican Republic & that girl tried to 'start something' with me & you followed her, *as she followed* ME to the bathroom upstairs. Usually I try to be 'on point', but in *that* moment I wasn't. *But you had my back*...and ever since then, you've had my heart also.

Another reason why I love you & appreciate you is because of **how similar we are.** *You make me not feel as strange as the mass population of people do* (indirectly). Growing up hard & fast ALSO, you *like myself,* don't have a *sense of entitlement* like most other grown adults & you don't 'expect' anyone to do anything for you. *You may ask people for help;* but that entitled-thinking that has corrupted the masses *isn't* in you (Thank God!). You know & realize that who & whatever *does* help you is a blessing from God! You know that God is Who you should look to & expect help from & that <u>HE</u> will lead you to what people <u>are</u> the Divine, 'open doors'.

I am grateful for your friendship, because you've been the barometer that has shown me that I don't have to *do* anything for someone or give someone *anything* & **they can** *still* **be my friend.** You've shown me that I can have a friend that really likes <u>me</u> & that the friendship is <u>not</u> based on what I can 'do' for them. I needed to

know this Truth & God used you to show it to me.
And I am grateful!

I hope you know that I forever want you to be an active part in my Life. You are just like family to me; just like my sister.–I hope that we always have a constant, continued, *fresh* relationship, that's always growing & becoming stronger. You are so special, rare & priceless. You are the iron that God uses to sharpen my iron. And *I never want* you to be absent in my world. I love you, Terr...and I just want to thank you so much, for loving someone like me.

- To Mary Alice Garland:
  There DEFINITELY...is not enough time to say thank you to you, Mary. I will try my best to be concise.

God told me to connect with you during a service when Apostle Clark was ministering about saving souls (10-22-15; Greensboro, NC) at a point in my life where I was:
1) walking in (chosen) spiritual isolationism &
2) **where I had <u>completely</u> given up on the goodness & genuineness of humanity.**

I'd experienced so many spiritually-*shady* things that I chose to believe that everyone had a *version* of fake-heartedness, *laced* with religion, within them. God used you, Mary, to break that mind-set off of me.

To me, **the most beautiful thing that God did in my**

Life *through knowing you* is that He broke the spirit of religion off of me. God used you to show me that it is:

1) <u>not</u> how a person *looks* or is *dressed* that denotes that God's Spirit is Living inside of them & 2) it is <u>not</u> the same criteria mentioned in #1 that reveals whether or not this same individual *is led in their heart by the Spirit of God* –therefore being a son of God.

It was your child-like faith & spiritual-*true*-hunger that PULLEDDDDDDD God's Fire OUT of me. –Fire that I didn't even know was THERE! God used YOU to bring out what He's been *wanting <u>out</u> of me* for so long; which is *His* Spirit & *His* Nature.

<u>I hid these things internally for so long, **not** being able to trust the spirits of those around me.</u> Then God *sent* you to our church...and the spiritual connection has forever, positively changed my Life.

I have looked at you & listened to you talk & realized how much *spiritual*-work I *still* need.

<u>Here you are:</u>
...this 'supposed-babe-in-Christ' and I realize that you *easily* do the things that Jesus asked us to do in His Word: like *believe* & *forgive!* I've been a witness to secretly, hateful-people *continuallyyyy* trying to undercut & destroy YOU & your *name* & <u>time</u> & <u>time</u> again...you've had God's heart & was WILLING to

forgive & restart again.

No grudge. No black-mail. –Just pure Love. And it's God manifesting Himself through you.

Just like people <u>OFTEN</u> *underestimate me* because of what I *look like* on the outside, people do the *very* **same** thing to you. People don't realize that God is *actually*...hiding inside of me, witnessing all that they do. And it's the same with you. People *stereotype* you (inside & outside of the 'church') & assume you are God-*less*, not realizing that God is <u>very</u> much **with** you & very much <u>in</u> you...

They don't realize at every opportune insight of faith –that you are continually laying aside the weights that have been spiritually dragging you down & away from God all of these years. I've seen the tremendous changes you've made in 20 months. It is remarkable. People think that because they don't '*see*', then it isn't so. **Knowing you...I know this is not true**.

Also, through knowing you, God WOKE up me to the realization that there <u>are</u> millions of people in the world that are similar to me; –that thought that there was no one in the 'church' that they could really relate to.
–*Feeling very spiritually 'different'* due to my personal story, my very, **NON-cookie-cutter history** that I en-countered BEFORE having met God (& even after

serving God). In our discussions, I realized that this is why God had me *endure*; so that I could be an encouragement to people that lived a very un-squeaky-clean life, as a testimony that you cannot judge a book by its cover. God can change & restore anyone!!!

Mary, you keep your spiritual-head up high & keep your heart bowed down low before the Lord, our Father-God. Every liar, deceiver, trickster, manipulator, witch, warlock, envious, pridefully-evil spirit that has & will ever try to come against you will ALWAYS be confounded BY THE LORD HIMSELF before your very eyes. **God said that He would be an Enemy to our enemies** (Exodus 23:22). This is why we...can smile at them. You focus on what God said...only.

Get your plans of actions together & shoot for the stars. The only force that can stop you is your own unbelief & lack of action(s). You know how to hear & sense God, now...so take your lessons...and PRO-DUCE!

I love you, Mary Garland. And although I know that you loved me in one of my hardest, spiritual places *by & through faith alone*, I am glad that you also, did not give up doing so. Your heart *in* God shows me...I **still** have a *ways* to go.

• To Shirelle Johnson: I still love you, even if it is hard to believe. I so wish I was wiser *then*. I am sorry. And I miss you still. I pray that you will loose all that has ever hindered you (seen & unseen) & that you will be safe, smart, successful & secure, always. Thanks for everything, Relle.

- To Shawnell Hawkins McCreary:
To the girl that let me live with her when she didn't even know me. We became sisters instantly & I hope that you will be the same forever. You are so strong & you deserve so much Love. I pray that you will always have true Love in your proximity. Thanks for believing in me & for ALWAYS asking me about the book! ☺

- **To my Grown, baby-girl Claudia Michelle**:
I want to set the record straight & let you know in print, forever to be charted, that I have ALWAYS loved you, Claudia. I do not know if anyone ever gave you the letter that I prayed that someone would let you read when you were of age old enough to try to 'understand'. I pray to God that you did not have a hard Life & that no one violated you in any way & that no one lied to you & made you believe that, me, your birth mother did not love you.

It broke my heart into a billion pieces when I gave you up for adoption when I was 15 years old.

With no ability to work, nor drive a car, with no help, no advice, nor assistance, being a product of a single-parent home myself, I didn't want you to suffer for my foolishness. I prayed & hoped that it was the best decision; I really did not know what else to do to offer you a better Life.

There is **not** enough time to write here...how my heart still immensely aches at the hole in my heart that represents your place; the constant-secret-sadness that plagues me –that I never speak of. Nothing & no one, Claudia, could ev-er...fill the hole that longs for your Presence. And I honestly wonder will I ever be whole without you in my Life.

The words here are for you alone; my heart **still** is shatter<u>ing</u>, with heart-shards scratching my throat as I now cry, wondering if I will ever see my baby again.

Claudia Michelle, I pray that you are alive & more than well. I hope, with everything that is within me, that we can be reconnected again. I want you to know, if you will accept me, if you will give me a chance to explain, I will never seek to hurt you. I **only** have ever wanted you in my Life; and I only gave you up for adoption because

Andy Cooper

I thought you deserved better than what I could provide which was only...love. A part of me died when I became separated from you.

I still cry, with the same, raw-intensity that I did when I left you with the adoption agency after 6 weeks of you breathing air. A **true** part of me died that day. And I became the walking-dead. And it is still, my sincere prayer, that one day I will be able to hold you in my arms again & cry *this* time, for the FIRST time in my Life...tears of joy. Please don't give up on me. I have ALWAYS loved you...regardless.

Foreword:

There are many manuscripts that have been written since the beginning of time that were intended to help the reader get *past* their current situation. The author more times than not, wrote the book from the standpoint of *having overcome*; they were OUT of the situation; they passed through the storm & came out on the *other* side to the place of victory & achievement.

I do not write this book from THAT standpoint. I am IN the situation(s) that you will read about. As I begin this task, I must admit that this will be **one** of ***the*** hardest things that I have ever had to do.

The prior, is a huge statement. *I have been through a lot of* **<u>heart</u>** *-breaking trials.* There have been many points in my life where I really wanted to lie down and die; to just give up due to the pain that was being felt emotionally, physically, mentally & spiritually.

I write this text according to **2 Chronicles 20:20**. This scripture states (according to the Women's Study Bible, New International Version) "*... **Have faith in the LORD your God & you will be upheld*** (supported, sustained, maintained, defended, endorsed, and encouraged)***; have faith in his prophets & you will be successful*** (triumphant, unbeaten & flourishing). "

My head-pastor, **Apostle Kelso Clark** of *Kingdom Power Worship Center*, Lynchburg, VA, prophesied twice (once in 2007 & yesterday 9-1-13) that my second book was going to be a bestseller. I do not know if he even remembers giving me the first prophesy years ago. I began to write another book earlier this year, thinking that *that* was the book God, the Great I AM, wanted me to write. On yesterday, Apostle Clark said that God wanted me to write about "The **TRAP**".

My pastors **Apostle Kelso Clark** & my personal, Life & Spiritual mentor **Apostle Jacqueline Clark** are true vessels consecrated unto God. They are true God-seekers & God-chasers. They skillfully operate in the *apostolic* & *prophetic* gifts & in the Calling of our Lord Christ Jesus, our Father God (Ephesians 4: 11-16;

1 Corinthians 12: 7-11). Being *apostolic* & *prophetic* simply means that they operate in the Authority of God, declaring God's Word of what *should* be and what *shall* be. They do this according *to* & *through* the *revelation* of the *Holy Spirit*; The Holy Spirit is the Power of God.

To tell *me* to write about "The **TRAP**" was a scary concept. It requires me to expose truth about myself: WHERE I've been, along with what I've DONE & THOUGHT. Who in the world likes telling on *themselves* when they've done wrong?!

My faith is definitely being put to the test. Do I *TRULY* believe 2 Chronicles 20:20? If I do, then I will write this book and publish it so that others may read it & be set free by acknowledgement & acceptance of the Truth –the Truth about themselves. In doing this, (*believing God* IN... my man & woman of God), exposing myself will help many others become free.

It is my prayer that God will take over my mind, body, soul & spirit **every** time I add to this text. – That God will draw out of the deep within me (my consciousness & my subconscious), the necessary material to bring extreme Glory to His *Wonderful*

Name...& restoration, healing & Wholeness to His people.

I pray that you will be honest with *yourself* in whatever way is necessary so that <u>you</u> may avoid "The **TRAP**" the enemy has waiting *especially* for *you* (James 1:14). If you've already walked into "The **TRAP**", I pray that you will take <u>by force</u> the Power God has given you, through Jesus' Blood and Love, to free *yourself.*

NOTE: You <u>do</u> need to be *under* the teaching of a **true** man &/or a **true** woman of God in order to spiritually '*see*', '*hear*', understand, & '*walk*' in apostolic (ordered) & prophetic (foresighted-directional) success.

Regardless of any hurt & deception that has entered your life (whether through your *own* decisions or the decisions of another), you ARE to be loved & do not deserve 'this' situation.
YOU...DESERVE...BETTER!

There is now NO more self-condemning!!! Jesus said so; this is why He died & rose again. Don't let

His death & Resurrection be in vain in YOUR life. *Again...* take by force the Power God has given you, through Jesus' Blood *and* Love, to free *yourself* from..."The **TRAP**".

Andy Cooper

Intention...

This book is intended to free everyone that has *considered*, been lured *by* &/or been caught *in* a **TRAP**.

TRAPs are set up by the enemy, the devil, the spiritual snake, the great deceiver & master manipulator, satan (lower-cased intentionally), Lucifier, the long-lasting enemy of God & enemy of God's people.

Know this: that you are beautiful/handsome, not only on the inside but also considerably on the outside! You are worth being treated with courtesy. The devil is an everlasting liar who *tries to make us think* that we have to tolerate situations & people that do not appreciate us, nor edify us! These lower-thoughts lead us into **TRAP**s.

I don't care what your **momma said**! I don't care what your **daddy** didn't **do**! I don't care who **left** you. We are not talking about who **died** or who wrongfully **molested** you. We are not focusing on who **abused** you or **hurt** you physically, verbally, financially, spiritually, socially, emotionally &/or mentally!

You are God's, The Great I AM's _chosen_ one; you were **handpicked** by God, to live a life that is _significantly_ different from all others. Your purpose in life is NOT to be abused; nor is it your purpose in life to be used!!! Your purpose is definitely NOT to conform to: the expectations, desires or 'fads' of other people. You survived those situations so that someone else could know that they too, have a chance...

It will FOREVER be the intent of the enemy, the devil, the spiritual snake, the great deceiver & master manipulator, satan, Lucifer, the long-lasting enemy of God & enemy of God's people, to try to sway **YOU** _off_ course, to make **YOU** operate in **complete**, low self-concept & self-condemnation. The devil will do so at _all_ costs...

The enemy's goal on a _daily basis_ is to get you to function in the _lesser_ state of yourself.

You were FEARFULLY made in the image & likeness of God (Genesis 1:26)! That means that *while* **living, thinking & breathing IN willingness, obedience & submission to God's Word, you have** complete **access to God's Power** (& permission to wield His Power)! – We are talking about the Power that God HIMSELF operates in!

God, Jesus, via His Holy Spirit has made YOU the authoritative power in the wondrous sphere called Earth! –Power that is in CONTROL OVER the enemy. But if you **don't** *realize* this nor accept the duty & call on your spiritual AND natural life...if you do not live UP to the expectation & realization of *this* Truth... then the enemy can have *permissive*, FREE COURSE over your life & EVERY thing that is connected to... you.

DECIDE TODAY that THIS situation is the last straw! This **TRAP** that YOU chose is 'the one that broke the camel's back'! Pick up your spiritual gall. And FIGHT the enemy back! Fight your way OUT of & away FROM the **TRAP**! Fight your way out *for*: your family, your heritage, your forefathers, and your lineage! Cancel the former thoughts within yourself! **Cease** from the old ways of belief. Who CARES what you did seconds ago?!

GOD, the Great I AM, is **THE <u>ONLY</u>** God of restoration & deliverance that is able, here RIGHT NOW, to set your SPIRIT free from the things that has *easily* bound you up until now. NO drug (illegal or prescription), no alcoholic concoction, no body part NOR movement, nothing you hear, no smell, no sound, no memory, no taste, no place, nor feeling can substitute for the continuous victory that your life CAN have in Christ Jesus!

*** **<u>NOW</u>** IS THE HOUR FOR BREAKING OUT OF THE *OLD* YOU! ***

The devil **<u>WILL</u>** continue to take you around in the same merry-go-round escapade that he HAS done, **day** after day, **month** after month, **year** after year, **generation** after generation, engagement after engagement, tour after tour...seeking to please people as you ignore yourself.

Don't you _recognize_ it?! Don't you see the repetitious trend(s)? Can't you NOW discover the negative *patterns* <u>your</u> life has taken, making decisions **outside of** God's Will?! This is why you picked up this book to begin with. **This is where <u>YOU</u> start to take control over <u>YOUR</u> life**.

Do not...be afraid.

Your spirit, which is your connection to God, has grown *tired*. The Holy Spirit, God's Operative Power & Will, is grieved, due to neglect...in YOU. Your soul longs for freedom! And it, your **soul**, will NEVER become free...until YOU <u>detest</u> **the things of old**, -*the <u>unfruitful patterns in your life</u>*, & <u>*yearnnnn*</u> for <u>the things of **new**</u> & be *relentless* in the pursuit of *positive* change. YOUR life and all that pertains to YOU, presently & futuristically, HEAVILY depends on YOUR spiritual <u>courage</u> & adamancy.

You are MORE than able to defy the wiles & objectives of the devil. I don't care WHAT your 'handlers' say.

Allow me to give you the keys & secrets that God is giving me.......to........................... "The **TRAP**".

Andy Cooper

MY TRUTH

It is best to know, that what I reveal in this book <u>is</u> <u>**for** you</u>.

I formerly was one of the most selfish people alive, *emotionally* & *mentally*. I would be **more** than willing to help you move, work on your team, go to your ceremony, give advice for your project, listen to your problems or praise report. But when it came to revealing my *own* personal thoughts, opinions, beliefs & desires, I was a master mind-manipulator. –One whose trust in others was scarce, primarily non-existent.

Being <u>**SO**</u> much smarter than I *look*, it was *easy* for me to fool others because **most everyone** would (& still *does actually*) underestimate my mind, aptitude & experiences. People would easily judge me based upon what <u>they</u> saw (see) & what <u>they</u> *thought* they knew & understood about me. And slyly, I would... ...**allow** them to...underestimate me.

For someone like me, who *was* who I was & *thought* what I thought...for ME... to tell YOU the truth about ME... is a sacrifice, FOR YOU, in honor of God.

God has made me realize that despite all of the hurt that I've encountered, there are MILLIONS of others that can relate & have experienced far **worse** than I have. God has shown me that I need to take <u>what I know</u>, apply it to my *own* life, & end selfishness by sharing with others so that we ALL can be set free.

Please...do not look at this as 'just another self help book'. I am **not** just another author. I was *chosen* for this. I was chosen for **you**, by God *Himself.* If I had it *my* way, you would <u>never</u> know the things about me that I will share with you. You would not even know my *name.* But if it will save a life, save a relationship, save a generation, &/or save a soul, then let my soul exposure begin. Pray for me, even ***now***, because my former, <u>**self**</u>-chosen, *foster*-father, the devil...is mad; because I am about to tell... the truth...about *him.*

Ezekiel 36:23

"I will show the holiness of My great Name, which has been profaned among the nations, the Name you have profaned among them. Then the nations will know that I AM the LORD, declares the Sovereign LORD. When I AM proved holy...through you...before their eyes."

Andy Cooper

INGREDIENTS (CHAPTERS) of THE TRAP

Ingredient 1: **Rejection**..2

Ingredient 2: **Insecurity** 35

Ingredient 3: **Low Self-Concept**.................................... 53

Ingredient 4: **Abandonment**..75

Ingredient 5: **Fear**.. 95

Ingredient 6: **Fantasy-Thinking** 110

Ingredient 7: **Settle-Mind-Set**......................................127

Ingredient 8: **Single-Parent Homes & Double-Parent Homes that Lack Parental-Unity** 145

Ingredient 9: **Immaturity**...165

Ingredient 10: **What Do You REALLY...Believe?!**.........185

Ingredient 11: **STIR** 214

Summary: ...the forsaken one 230

INGREDIENT ONE

Rejection

Rejection: (the root word 'reject', defined as) one that has been discarded or refused.

<u>**Know this**</u>: <u>that with any **demonic recipe**, the enemy's **main** ingredient in attempting to destroy *your* life is **rejection**</u>. The devil, the evil one, will incite rejection into your life as *early* as possible. If the enemy can have his way, he will make sure that rejection is a part of your *every* memory, *especially* the early ones.

How did rejection begin in my life?

As with millions of others, rejection first began with my biological father. He & my mother separated when I was 2 years old. To give him some benefit of doubt, as far as I am aware of, my father has made no attempt to reach out to me. And I am currently 34 years old as I write this.

As a child, I did not understand why I did not have a father around. Finally at the age of 7 years old, I inquired my mother as to the reason. She gave me her explanation, which considering the situation, was as 'politically correct' as possible. She attempted to give me mere facts, *abandoning* insertion of *her* feelings in her recollection of events that led to us being a single-parent home.

(I congratulate her; most parents take the opportunity to 'bad-mouth' the other parent due to bitterness & rejection. My mom did not claim that chance.)

At the end of revealing the reason to our, then, current circumstance, I ascertained that regardless of *what* my mother & father's relationship *was* or was *not*, that had **nothing** to do with why he was not a part of MY life. I decided at 7 years of age that he officially did not care about me. <u>**This**</u>**... was the root of rejection in my life.**

UNDERSTAND:

You MUST uncover/discover & realize what the <u>root</u> of rejection is in <u>*your*</u> life.

You must uncover the shady details, those sore places <u>in your soul</u> that you do not want to think about. Honestly speaking, I delayed in even *beginning* this ingredient/chapter because I simply did not want to *think* about or *deal* with this situation. It **hurts** to recognize that someone that *should* have loved you and cared for you did not deem doing these things as important; that they were 'able' to go on & live their life *as if you didn't exist,* when **they** were an integral part in even *creating* you (imagine big-eyed emoji inserted here). (For the doubters, my father had access to my mother's people. If he wanted to associate with me, this could have been communicated to other relatives besides my mother.)

<u>The **root** of rejection</u> is the pinnacle point where everything else, (all other negative mind-sets, bad decisions & poor perceptions) *<u>begins being **filtered** through</u>* rejection TO your mind & your soul. **Your self-esteem & self-confidence is** slowly diminished **when the <u>root of rejection</u> is hidden & untreated.** *The root grows invisibly larger & stronger under-*

neath the foundation of... you.

Due to not having a father around, I never learned
what every little girl should & NEEDS to know:
that she is pretty, adorable & to be loved appropri-
*ately **only** because she is who she is.* –Loved *merely*
because she is unique, special & because she **exists**.
Without a foundational male role-model (acting as a
<u>full</u>-time father figure) teaching and showing her
innocent-love, the little girl grows up, falling prey
to the inceptive, lifestyle suggestions that this
<u>worldly</u> <u>media</u> offers.

The inceptive, lifestyle suggestions used in worldly
media are tools and tactics influenced by the evil
one, the devil. –Worldly Media uses tools & tactics
that are intended to *skew* the **proper** projections of
self that we are to emulate as God's images & God's
likenesses in the earth. (Genesis 1:26-28; 2 Corinthians 4:6-7)

The devil begins to insert implications into our
hearts & minds that:
...we are not pretty or handsome enough, that we
are not strong enough, that we are not smart

*enough, that we are not talented enough, that we are not the right size, that we do not have the right skin tone, that we do not come from or live in the right place, that we do not talk the right way, that we do not have nice hair, we do not know the right people &/or connections, that we are not the right height, that we do not have enough money, that we do not have the right clothes or shoes, that we are not in the right position in life, that we do not hang out in the right places, that we do not act the right way...*all of these are the 'supposed' reasons that we are not popular, properly pursued, sought after, admired, *treasured,* respected &/or loved.

This little girl (or boy), with the lack of foundational teaching of *appropriate exchanges* of love, falls into the **TRAP**(s) that *rejection...initially...*set.

Rejection & submission to the correlating, *uncorrected* thoughts <u>that come *with* rejection</u>, set the little girl (or boy) up to think (subconsciously) that she/he must 'do' things in order to receive attention & affection. Once she/he *gets* attention, she/he must follow up with '**<u>doing</u>**' what is requested of her/him so that she/he can 'acquire' what the world has transmitted (through TV, internet, social media, movies, and magazines) is love, **albeit false love.**

Worldly-media suggestions tell little girls & boys through subliminal & apparent messages (*millions* of times a day), that sex(iness), lewdness, flirtation & money are the 'keys' to get what you want. You have to look the 'right' way & 'play' the right part in order to 'get' what it is that you long for.

Hence, the results of: fad-like dressing *(tights looking like jean-pantyhose, shorts that resemble panties, men wearing pants so tight that it shows the imprint of their genitalia, shirts showing cleavage or bras completely seen through the shirt, ultimate short skirts or skirts with splits up to the buttcrack, see-through clothes or lack of clothes at all, men wearing pants <u>below</u> their belt line, even UNDER the butt-cheeks!!!)*, teen & pre-teen pregnancies, youth drug addicts & alcoholics, entry into gangs, hustlers, 'slingers' (drug dealers), orgies, the making of woman-beaters, introductions to bi-sexuality, homosexuality & lesbianism, introductions to prostitution... the list can actually go on.

The youth <u>find it hard to believe</u> that they are **deserving** of love without giving... their bodies... up to some... unholy cause. They **feel <u>obligated</u>**...they feel that they have to 'put in work' to get loyalty & respect. This is what the world teaches; this is **not** God's way, according to *His* Word, *His* Integrity, & *His* Nature.

Christ Jesus first Loved us. He Loved us when we didn't know Him, didn't love Him, nor did we love ourselves! (1 John 4: 9-19)

So the negative, downward spiral continues; one bad decision leads to another. One heart-break leads to **more** insecurity. *Insecurity* leads to more *personality suffocation, attempting*...to be like what you *think* you **have** to be like, <u>trying to attain *inaccurate-imitations*</u> of the (appropriate) love you **never** *initially* **knew!!!** (Please meditate on this prior statement.)

The more you try, the more you fail, the more pain that enters your life. You turn to what the world (once again) offers as medicine, another **TRAP:**

drugs and alcohol, to soothe the secret, silent, internal screams & tears. NOW you've passed through the **TRAP**s of rejection, low self-esteem, low self-worth & emotional neglect (with all of the accompanying bruises, wounds and scars) into the <u>new</u> **TRAP**s of fear & doubt.

The TRAPs of fear & doubt are the two TRAPs that the devil longs to lead you to. <u>The devil knows that once you enter into **fear** & **doubt**, that it will take God Himself to free you out of them.</u>

Just think about it...what are you really afraid of? – The thing(s) that you haven't *even* told your spouse/best friend... - The thing(s) that you are so fearful over that you don't even allow yourself to meditate thoughts *towards*? More than likely these things require action from *you*...somehow.

-Actions from you...that will initiate change in your life & quite possibly in the lives of many others (i.e. me writing this book). Even MORE likely, the thing that you fear or doubt is worth accomplishing (!); it is something that the enemy does not WANT you to do! *Why*? Because your action(s) will set <u>you</u> free & bring <u>God</u> glory!

WHATTTTTTTTTTTTTT?!
Yes! This...is...the...purpose...of...the devil's...**TRAP**s! –To keep you AWAY from what is the
BEST intention for your Life. –To keep you from
what <u>God</u> **planned** for your Life.

**God has a pre-determined destiny for *all* of our
Lives.** –Even for the possibly, spiritually-
schizophrenic, homeless man, with inadequate help,
that *you* like calling a 'bum' &/or crazy. <u>All of our
paths</u> that lead to destiny & promotional prosperity
(in mind, in body, in spirit & in soul) are paths that
God *orchestrated* to bring Glory to His Name
(through us!); so that the entire earth may know
that God, The Great I AM, <u>IS</u> alive, well, AND...that
He Rules & Reigns Supreme!

The devil, called the enemy for **<u>a reason</u>**, is against
God & feels that the only way that he can 'get back'
at God (since the devil has no power or authority over
God, **OR** God's people) is to *steal, kill* & *destroy* the
lives of God's people, by *tricking* them to use their
<u>OWN</u> **God**-given Power *against themselves*. (John
10:10)

The enemy knows that *rejection* leads to *fear* &
doubt. And that *fear* & *doubt* will keep you *improp-*

erly unconnected to God (God being our Source of All). **Without** <u>FAITH</u>...it is IMPOSSIBLE to please God! (Hebrews 11: 6) If we are not properly connected to God (through our genuine heart-<u>faith</u>), then we cannot receive *help* from God for our souls, nor guaranteed help for our lives (*5 components of the soul*: the <u>mind</u>, the <u>will</u>, the <u>intellect</u>, the <u>imagination</u> & the <u>emotions</u> of yourself).

God, being ALL-Powerful, can send us help when we are in the time of trouble (Psalm 46: 1, 7, 10), but unless we are freed from the (TRAP of...) old mindset(s) that got us **to** that troubled position in the *first* place; our lives will be that of a crazy person living on a huge merry-go-round expecting to see different sites!

<u>Various Rejection Thoughts</u>: "*I am not worth love. I* **have** *to have sex with her (or him) or else they will leave me & go be with someone else. I* **have** *to act this way or dress this way, otherwise they won't like me & they won't be my friend anymore, nor hang out with me anymore. I* **have** *to steal these items because they are counting on me to come through <u>for</u>*

*them. It's what everyone (now) expects out of me. How can I go back? I do not want to be alone or un-liked. <u>Everyone else</u> left me. If I sleep with married people then I don't have to worry about false com-mitment. I already know they can't stay with me. Guys/girls only want me for my body &/or my mon-ey anyway. The <u>only</u> compliments or interest that I receive pertain to my physical attributes or posses-sions. No one shows interest in my thoughts or cares about what's in my heart or what is connected to my soul! People only want to use me for what they can get out of me anyway...inside & outside of the 'church'. He/she is just trying to be nice to me so that they can try to take 'my place'. Nobody else thought that my feelings mattered. If I really 'be me', or the <u>new</u> me that I want to be, <u>who</u> will ac-cept me? The people that rejected me didn't like the 'me' I **<u>naturally</u>** was; how am I to believe that the re-al me will be liked **now**? I do not even know who the new, **real** me is!!!'*

....

Once again, there was a delay (unknown to you) in the writing of this ingredient/chapter. After the last sentence of the last paragraph, I quit writing for about 6 weeks. I can use different excuses of being busy with other Kingdom assignments, the handling of family concerns, working of mandatory overtime at work, all of which are variations of the Truth. But the **deep Truth**...is that it became *hard*.

It was hard realizing that at 34 years old, I am actually **STILL** dealing with the root of rejection.

–Realizing (in hind-sight) that for the last 3 ½ years of my Life, I was involved with someone that *emotionally* was not involved with me, yet **incessantly** *craved* me *physically*. A man that was content on sleeping with me, **KNOWING ABSOLUTELY...** that I was <u>in</u> Love with him...<u>not</u> concerning himself with my emotional <u>or</u> spiritual well-being...WHILE...sleeping with God knows HOW many *other* women simultaneously. Even as I am typing this, tears are beginning to form & fluently flow from my eyes.

But...we wrestle not against flesh and blood, God's Word says (Ephesians 6:12-18). The man that kept his heart at bay, while he kept his penis in close proximity...was only a tool, a tactic that the devil had been using to *deepen* my hurt(s) that was suppressed & <u>un</u>addressed for decades.

The devil *knew* that at 30-something years old, that regardless of how strong people *perceive* me to be, that in essence I was still that little, 4 year old girl with no daddy loving her and not understanding *why he*, didn't want to be around (me). –And due to that un-removed root of rejection, I found myself, **once again**, settling for *pretend*-love & counterfeit-affection & performing God-less acts to have...what *wasn't*...even...real.

The devil is so **evil**, so crude, that he would even cause men that *knew* that their hearts <u>weren't</u> compassionately connected to my well-being, to tell me to call *them* 'daddy' during those '*intimate*' moments...
  It was the ***devil*** asking me, <u>*through them*</u>, to call *him...* 'daddy'.

The devil ... –reverberating in my psyche that: '*yes, Andrea. I'm using flesh/carnal tendencies to cause you to hurt <u>yourself</u>. I am influencing you to lay your true, God-like Nature aside (Genesis 1:26, 27). The root of rejection is so invisibly wrapped* *around your heart. Your **pathetic** longing is an easy target for me and...FOR ANY man that I chose to use to '**get**' you. **All** we have to do is: ½ way pretend to spend time with you. We don't even have to tell you that we love you. And even IF we DID tell you that we love you, it wouldn't be true. And the **really** sad part: is that you know this <u>all</u> to be true.'*

Being in this 3 ½ year incident *(can I call it a relationship when in hind-sight there was no nurturing, nor reciprocated love, outside of physical oneness?!)*, I realized at <u>the end</u> of the manipulation, confusion & hurt, (after years of trying to be empathetic concerning '*his schedule*'), that the **Truth**...was that he was a human-chameleon that lived **countless**, *versionssssss* of lives & *concealed* (<u>q</u>uite SUC-CESSFULLY) **various** personas with VARIOUS people, in order to maintain his selfish, deceptive, <u>sexual</u> motives & goals...<u>ALL</u> OF WHICH, were hidden, **even** from those *closest* to him.

–To have the truth exposed (that I was getting '*played*')...& revealed to me (through God's Divine orchestration!), confirming ALLLLLL the ques-

tions that I posed through the duration of my encounter with this person--- **it**...*broke*... **me**. *I believed that this was a good man.* I thought his 'good
deeds' were indicative of what his secret-heart con-
tained (inaccurately believing it was true-Love).

I thought that he was '**distant**' sometimes because,
like myself, he'd been hurt & was *afraid* to *fully* let
go & *truly* love. I thought he was a humanitarian;
someone that could & *would* **finally** love me *correct-
ly.* I thought that he cared about what was *best* for
me, whole-heartedly.

I was too blinded with rejection-issues to realize
that this man was 100%-<u>incapable</u> of Loving me *appropriately.* His capacity for **True**-Love was *under
par. He was ONLY <u>gifted in the forgery & imitation
of Love.</u> Appropriate* Love comes from
God...because God <u>IS</u> Love.

<u>Best described</u>:
...the Truth of me being *'<u>one</u> of many women',* an
<u>unknown</u>, *secret*-number in an *unseen* line... it **shat-
tered** me. Shards of me remained. My head & heart
hurt **so** incredibly bad for **MONTHS** at a time

(which turned into 2 ½ *additional* years), that I just wanted to lie down & **never** get up *again*. That is <u>not</u> a 'drama-queen' statement...that is a truthful reality. (And for the record: due to rejection-issues, I chose fornication as a 'down-payment' for 'hopeful' love; **knowing** full-well, fornication is OUT of God's Will.

 –Which is why I only reaped *lust* & grief, in return.)

'*Depression*'isn't qualifiably the word that came 'over' me.

It was as if my *soul* died (my mind, will, intellect, imagination, & emotions). The ONLY reason I was even able to GET UP at ANY moment was because the HOLY SPIRIT took over my body!

...**TRULY!!!!!!!!** I felt like a human weight without desire or self-initiative for movement. I could *hardly* think, eat, talk, walk, sleep &/or breathe without breaking out into *painful* tears (**tears** that factually **hurt** when exiting my ducts). I felt like I was <u>literally</u>, *emotionally* dying. ...*And I kept it* **<u>all</u>** *to myself...*

I kept this 'relationship' a secret from family & friends 'to make sure that it was something that God wanted to *endorse'*---ultimately I didn't want to 'look' like a fool (how unwise, *Andy!*); ...no one knew about it, so I didn't feel comfortable enough to share my pain. After all, I should have '<u>*known*</u>' ...better.

I always thought that I would be the one to be able to recognize the 'wolf'. I always thought that I would be able to see his wolf-tail. I realize **now**...that the **true** 'wolf'...*hides* his wolf-tail...in his **heart**.

"HOW, Andy?! How could you **continue** to be so *stupid"*, I ask myself...
–So desperate (yuck), so needy, so *hungry* for *Love*, that you would **continually** accept a **false ideal**, ignoring actions, & believing his *lying* words.

I accepted a man that *socially* was everything that one should want: a Christ Jesus believer, a working man, a church-goer, kind-hearted, smart, funny, family-oriented, whatever-have-you. But he offered <u>no</u> commitment; only *vagueness, vacillating closeness, perplexity, restrained-mental intimacy,* nonchalant, frequent, undetermined episodes of **coldness**, ONLY...to be 'sweet & nice' when wanting to '*see*'...me again. "HOW, Andy?! How could you **continue** to be so *stupid?*"

Like a devoted, trained dog, I would go back *time* & *time* again, to offer '***me***', *sacrificing* dignity & *sacrificing* self- respect, *hoping*...that *this* would 'prove' how much I Loved and cared for him.

Once realizing the Truth of how the last 3+ years **was an ultimate & absolute lie**, a spiritual sham (unbeknownst to me, from the very beginning), *of course*...Life...did not pause so that I could 'get myself together'. Life continued on.

Requests were still made of me. Deadlines were still enacted. Demands were still expected. Bills were still punctual. There was no 'time' for me to grieve & have a 'moment'. As mentioned prior, this went on for months, which actually led to years! To seek 'relief', I pried open & got *into* a familiar, almost dusty **TRAP**: of *drugs & alcohol.*

I knew in times past, that **alcohol** could: soothe &
ease & **drugs**: could temporarily lessen & numb the
pain. The self-destruction of using drugs & alcohol
never seemed to matter before; when you are just
'trying to get through'. I knew & understood the
immediate effects (*not the eventual effects*). I felt
like it was my only option at an 'attempt' at achiev-
ing sanity in a <u>very</u>, **demanding** life. *Every sector* of
my Life was ***pressing*** me...for some sort of action
that I had **zero initiative** for. After 4 months of internal dying, <u>**something**</u> had to give.

So I went back to my former substance-lovers, the
ones that wiped my tears & kissed me on the cheeks
when sad: weed, pills, alcohol. I instituted them in
my daily routine. *Thankfully* still possessing some
sort of responsibility, I didn't do anything before
going to work. But IMMEDIATELY UPON DE-
PARTING WORK, I would go home & 'zone out'.
I'd get <u>scary</u>-high (**true** weed-smokers & ex-weed
smokers know what I am talking about; *not* the so-
cial/recreational-smokers) trying to 'drown' out
thoughts & have a moment of 'chill'. While doing
so, I would drink alcohol until I felt sluggish.

At the times when I had to go to church (**YES!** Can you believe a Kingdom-of God-citizen was **doing these** things?!?), (my attendance generally was 2-4 days a week, depending on what was going on), I would get high, drink, then 'pop' pills so I could 'calm' down, then drink double Colombian coffees so that I wouldn't fall asleep in church. By the time I GOT *to* church, I was like a nervous, **numb** *zombie*. I would sit like a statue, barely blinking, yet my hands & heart would be shaking & racing. One time someone asked me to send a text to someone & I couldn't do it because my hands were quivering so badly. When sitting, I would usually hold my hands together, as *most* people do when they sit. My substance abuse was pretty much undetected, *along* with my pain.

SO...I followed this 'smoke, drink, pop, Colombian-coffee' routine...for over a year. Sadly & *ironically*, as far as I know, the only **evident** thing that suffered during this time was my production concerning **Kingdom**-business (my duties at church).

At the time, I was an adjutant or an armorbearer for my pastor/Life Coach (wife of the head pastor), as well as, the personal administrative assistant to both head-pastors. I was constantly making mistakes, forgetting things, not following up, and doing things wrong or incompletely. I was living in **perpetual** fear & **constant** anxiety over getting 'in trouble' with my pastors, <u>ON TOP OF</u> the hurt & pain that I was *already* trying to mask. *Yet...* every time...I would show up, after my smoke-drink-pop-coffee session, with my (as an associate of mine says) "pasted, beauty-pageant smile", hiding the 'shakes', saying the 'right' things, hoping that people would talk to me as **least** as possible.

Long story shortened, God exposed the situation to my head-pastors through the working of the Holy Spirit. (You better **know** that Yahweh is alive & well & moves & sees & knows ALL things! If you DON'T know, ask someone about Him that KNOWS Him!) The Holy Spirit did it while I was out of town for two weeks. During those two weeks, I was absolutely struggling with coming back home. If my friend said that I could stay with her, I would have left eve-ry**thing** & every **one** behind...*quite easily*, with no real explanation offered. When I came home & realized the Truth was exposed, I wanted to run away.

As far as church duties, I was 'sat down' (released from assignments/responsibilities), restored (repositioned) & 'sat down' **again** 3 months later. I continued to dabble back & forth with the smoke-drink-pop-coffee sessions.

---*Now*, I've let it all go...so that I can acknowledge & accept the Truth, with NO mask, NOR running from the **Truth** that *stings*. God is right NOW working on me, so that YOU can know how He wants to work on you.

One **TRAP** to the next **TRAP**...the devil wants us to play 'hop-scotch' with his **TRAP**s like mice on pogo-sticks trying to get away from lions. –Hilariously futile, getting *nowhere* fast.

This is how I could stay in a *former* relationship (when I was *much* younger) with a man that told me all day long that he loved me, yet physically, mentally, emotionally, verbally, socially, spiritually & financially abused me. He tried to manipulate my mind & emotions at **every** opportune moment. He tried to make me think that I was crazy & not in control of my own thoughts.

This *same* man broke 3 of my fingers on 3 *different* occasions. He hit me, choked me, pushed me, and called me every name in & under 'the book' (even in front of one of his own family members). He kicked my door in (twice, **off** the hinges), punched holes in my walls, followed me in unmarked cars, socially bullied me into being scared to look at the opposite sex in the face, embarrassed me at work in front of co-workers...but in all of this....he '*loved*' me.

It was *my* fault, *he said*, that he acted 'that' way. I didn't 'understand' how much he *cared*, *he said*. He would get so angry that he didn't know what to do sometimes, *he said*. – But that he couldn't live without me & that he would kill himself if I left him, *he said*. On many occasions, *he said* he was going to get counseling. But he *needed me* to **believe** in him, believe in *his* love.
And with no real, <u>deciphering</u> skills of what <u>real</u>
Love *should* be, I stayed and tried year, after year, after year, after year, after year...

–One relationship extreme to the *other* extreme...no happy medium.

And ironically...the *first* man mentioned to you, before this last man, who kept his heart, **<u>not</u>** his penis distant from me, told me **to my face**, that he can SEE why someone would "put their hands on me"......the man that I *longed* to have love me would *think* **&** *say*...something like that(?!). **Yes!** An **overdue reality check** was needed for me.

All of this is a true parents' nightmare. Who would ever want to imagine that their daughter or son was subjecting themselves to being **used** in **any** way, shape or form, because their child longed so *desperately* to receive Love & affection?

An associate of mine mentioned to me that their son wanted to know what would be something nice that he could purchase for a female that he was 'trying to get to *like* him'. I told this person, "**You have to nip that mindset in the bud!** You must teach your son **NOW** that if a woman is not going to want or Love him ONLY because of WHO he is, and **not** what he can *do* for her, then that woman is **not** worth being with AT ALL. Her love, time and attention will **only** be superficial. And he needs to **know** & understand this!"

But it's seen *every* day!

And society/social media *encourages* it.

Parents & teachers are <u>too</u> desensitized & <u>too</u> task-oriented to realize that *their* **child is a** *perfect* **candidate for emotional & physical perversion.** –

*The...*devil's playground intended to destroy your physical & spiritual lineage for **generations** to come. And this is all attributed to the ROOT of rejection, whether **seen** or unseen; whether **known** or unknown.

God told me through His Holy Spirit one morning when getting ready for work that: "**People who are <u>insecure are liars</u>; because they don't have the courage to stand up for what is <u>Truth</u>**..." A VERY humbling statement; it hit me like a ton of bricks. ' *What are you* **<u>saying,</u>** *God? Am* **<u>I</u>** *insecure?*'

Yes.

I have been subconsciously insecure for most of my existence & this insecurity that was **instilled** by the initial & subsequent rejection(s), *fostered* this undisclosed, insecure mindset within me. *Insecurity* (birthed through unresolved rejection) is that which has caused me to subject *myself* to inadequate treatment, **time** & time again, **situation** after situation, **year** after year, for the last **20** years.

I know...that as parents, you have odd work hours, committee responsibilities, massive bills, personal trials & concerns; but all of these things <u>should</u> **<u>not</u> <u>take precedence</u>** over making sure that your child is receiving sufficient nurturing & that *your* relationship with them is being fostered. Provision & material possessions *do not replace* time spent in getting to know *them*, how & WHAT they think, feel or know (or DON'T know!).

NOT knowing what is in *their* heart & in *their* mind is how you **allow** them to be swayed away (...eventually) by the evil one, -the devil & his **emotional** *lures*. How *else* can you combat the illicit suggestions presented to them, if you don't even know **who** they are, **what** it is that they face, or what they are **prone** to accept **or** *believe, especially* in times of peer-pressure (the devil's fire)?

Without constructive cultivation of conversation, how do you **know** whether they will *suitably* deflect negative offerings to alternative lifestyles & choices? It is very dangerous, the child that is left to entertain *themselves* in the house with or without you in it, because *you* must sleep, work, do assignments &/or take care of whatever duty you've obligated *your*self *to*. This creates *inadvertent* rejection.

I am not bashing your parental skills.
I am only **announcing** the need for relationship,
-time _well_ spent & **invested** (*not* your time '*left*-overs'). Relationships require time spent talking, listening, learning, helping, nurturing, understanding & Loving *each other*. This needs to be done before they are pre-teens, *if* possible.

After becoming pre-teens, they've been **conditioned** & predisposed to keeping their thoughts **to themselves** & it will be *somewhat* difficult to 'pry' the answers from them to the questions that you _now_ possess. The 'one word' answers (from them) ensue. The gap (emotionally) between you & them broadens & ultimately you are strangers living under the same roof.

ALL OF WHICH, is what the devil wants ANY-WAY!!!!!
he (lower-cased intentionally) **wants you to be too busy**

to pay attention to your child or to spend quality time talking, laughing with & Loving them. The devil wants the TV, the Internet, video games, FaceBook, Twitter, Snapchat, chat rooms, Instagram, friends & magazines to substitute **your** influence in the Life of *your* child **or...to BECOME** *your* **OWN, personal distraction** concerning...your child(ren)! These arenas are all avenues that the devil spews his godless-venom through, in attempts to infect their (your) spirit and rationale.

If the devil can't kill them, which he will **undoubtedly** *try* to do, he wants them to end up like I recently was: a full-grown adult, *feeling pressured to the max*, living a life **COMPLETELY** unsatisfied, living & doing things **only** trying to please people at *church* & *work*, wondering how long the wait for soul-fulfillment will be.

–Knowing that the enemy has his **TRAP**s WD-40'd up, waiting on me to fall prey to depression, disappointment & discouragement, *once* again.

If the devil cannot kill you or your seed, he is **equally** happy with making sure that you do not operate in God's Power that Jesus died & was Resurrected for you (us) to have access to. The enemy is fine with you staying in a pitiful, dark pit, secret or not. As long as you <u>aren't</u> producing Glory for Yahweh, the Great I AM...the devil couldn't give two hoots.

The evil one doesn't want you to be like the NEW me that is AWAKENING to righteousness, - realizing that I <u>do not</u>...have to be an **ejaculation-bag** for the devil's skilled males; spiritually-trained men <u>who AIM to *purposely* **deceive** me</u> (and women who are secretly like me) with the '*prospect*'...of '*possible*' 'love'. These demonically-used-prophetically-trained men are experts at feeding & fueling false dreams.

–The devil doesn't want us to realize these same type of men/& **women** (they have different faces/genders, but the same, secretive-evil nature) are scandalous-spiritual liars that want us fascinated & deluded with mental-implantations of suggestive-malarkey that will <u>never</u> be.

I had to awaken fully & know: regardless of *what* & *who* failed to recognize my worth <u>*my entire*</u> life, it does not mean that I am not valuable. That the hurts, the pains, the rejections, the sufferings, the tears, the **years** of torment & grief, they all have an eventual, GOOD, & GLORIOUS Purpose (Romans 8:28).

What else can be said to convince you of the need to deal with *rejection* (in <u>YOUR</u> Life & the Lives of your seed)? –The need of discovering the *original* root of rejection that led to all the other 'foggy' decisions that you made afterward. **The uncovered root of rejection runs deep.**

More than likely you don't even know where to begin OR it's too painful to even look back! Get with an anointed, God-seeking, holy-living, consecrated, *sanctified,* humble, **<u>TRUE</u>** (emphasis on 'TRUE') man or woman of God that can help you **realize** the root of rejection in your *own* life (Proverbs 20:5).

Pray to the Holy Spirit to give you supernatural discernment to **appropriately** test spirits (1 John 4:1), so that you can know if the pastor/leader you are trying to get to know (if you do not have a trusted pastor *already*) has the TRUE heart of God & <u>**that they are NOT trying to spiritually-molest you**</u> (physically, mentally, emotionally, financially, spiritually &/or socially).

Prepare yourself, because the Truth might hurt you or even *anger* you. It will be like ripping off an old scar, exposing the *original* wound that you've subconsciously learned to cover up &/or become numb to. But *after* wound-exposure for some time now, let me let **you** know, *eventually* the pain *lessens* through recognition, responsiveness, realizing & receiving of THE TRUTH. We MUST come to ACCEPT the Truth, *even* if we do not like it!

It's the **Truth** that we've run from.
It's the Truth...that we've discarded. It's the lack of Truth in our Lives & in foundations of decisions that leaves us feeling powerless & out of control.

BUT...it is a NEW day, A NEW dawn. Morning has come *after* your mourning! YOU **ARE** TO BE LOVED, sweet person of God. Whoever chose to leave you or hurt you, was not ABLE to personally love nor **know** the full, *true* meaning of Love, - which **IS** God. (1 John 4:7)

Love IS NOT LOVE, if they do not love you **like God loves you**, (which is without impure motives or desires)!

Bottom-line, hands-down! No exceptions, no ifs, ands or buts!

The enemy <u>will</u> *try* to lie to you & make you think that 'there are exceptions to the way that people love' or 'everybody is different', blah-zay-blah... These are lies from the pits of hell.

God **is** Love, ***only***! If the love *offered* is not of God, & the offered love doesn't have God's Fragrance or God's Character or God's Integrity attached to it, **<u>then it is a forged counterfeit</u>**, determined & *positioned* to subtly deceive you into spiritual stagnation & *eventual* self-destruction.

It's time to look back, buddy.
You are not alone in the discovery-process. God, Christ Jesus, The Holy Spirit are there *with* you, holding your heart <u>&</u> your hand. And me also...I am *here* praying with and *for* you... that <u>**we**</u> come out *together*, <u>**FULLY**</u> whole, and **finally** living on top, forever!

We DO have the victory. God <u>has</u> our back!
We **finally** have to let 'it' go (the roots of rejection),

trust *God's Word* & <u>really</u> work our faith...***truly***, this time...not with religion; not with the bondage of the expectations of people; but with heart-connected action to God's Word & Holy Spirit.

Team up with God today; He is ready to start (& complete) your process of healing; so that He can usher you (us) to the next, **higher** dimension in Life...But we can't go to the next dimension of Life in God, with a deep, thick-rejection-root keeping us grounded to the *past*.

Expose & destroy the roots of rejection in our Lives, Christ Jesus!
–Through and by Your All Powerful, Holy Spirit, Father God. We spiritually hold Your Hand & give You our hearts & grant You *permission* to begin the process that will make us spiritually Whole. We thank and praise You now in advance...IT <u>IS</u>...SO!!

Insecurity

WHOA!

Once again, it's been some time since I've written, oh *valued* one. I went back to see where we were last in written prose...and wooooooo! What a mighty Word from the Lord! I must admit that I received **renewed** help, once again. I hope that you received help from the Lord, as well!!!

Admittingly, it's been a while since writing because of this current chapter: ***Insecurity***. I hope that you do not mind my honesty & the breaking down of writing sessions with you. But as stated in the beginning, God is working me THROUGH *this*...AS...I am writing. I have not already overcome these situations: I am overcoming them now. So this book being shared with you is very spiritually personal. And you should know that you are not alone in this feat. We are going through this (with God) *together.*

Why ---was it difficult for me to begin writing about insecurity? I am not sure about you, but I am not aware of many people that are willing to openly admit that they are insecure about **any**thing. Ultimately, this is the reason: discomfort.

The delay resulted because I wasn't willing to *even* touch the subject. The thought at thinking of insecurity made me spiritually & emotionally **tense.** And I decided to leave it alone for a moment. But now, I am ready to hold God's Hand & go further still. (sigh)

I've learned that we need to make sure that we understand what seems to be simple because *sometimes* our version of understanding may be incomplete. Therefore, let us look at the definition of insecurity.

INSECURITY (n): 1) uncertainty or anxiety about **oneself**; lack of confidence.

2) the state of being open to danger or threat; lack of protection.

Will you say, "WHOAAAA!" with me?!

Considering these two definitions, I must be honest with God, you & myself & say that I have been insecure the majority of my life. **It is appropriate to realize that rejection & the root(s) of rejection breeds insecurity.**

It is somewhat of an egotistical-insult to realize that the inner, hidden part of my nature has an undertone of insecurity. If you were to know me as some that are close to me, 'insecure' would be the very LAST word that you'd use to describe me. I am extremely bold, even to the point of appearing insolent. I can be very confrontational; yet I am spiritually & naturally sensitive. I am considerate; although it's *not* hard for me to say no. And I definitely am not a push-over. To me, *I thought* that insecure people are weak-hearted & weak-minded.

So for me to be so 'sturdy' & 'strong', how can I be insecure?!

In ingredient/chapter 1, I told you that God spoke to me concerning insecurity one day, as I was getting ready for work. And it was VERY much 'out of the blue' when He spoke to me. I was not worshipping or praising Him, nor praying, that I can recall. God just said to me (Nov. 2013 –almost a year ago! – Now it is Oct. 2014), "**People who are insecure are liars; because they don't have the courage to stand up for what is Truth...**" As stated before, this is a very humbling statement that hit me like a ton of bricks. '*What are you* saying *God? Am I insecure?*'

So, self-analyzation must be performed.

"Are there moments in your life, *Andy*, where you've been tempted to lie (to not tell the Truth), because you thought that telling the truth would make matters worse?" Being able to answer yes to this question means that in those moments that I have thought of, I was operating in insecurity.

INSECURITY (n): 1) uncertainty or anxiety about **oneself**; lack of confidence.

2) the state of being open to danger or threat; lack of protection.

We think that if our reasons are GOOD enough (self-rationalized as justifiable), then it is okay for us to lie. This is even more true when we convince ourselves that we 'have' to lie in order to **protect** those we say (or feel) that we love &/or care for.

But the lie is really about *us*. We do not possess the courage to stand up for what IS True, so we lie – which reveals our insecure nature.

I KNOWWWWWWWWWWWWWWW...it's a lot to swallow. It is a lot to take in. Why do you think that I stopped writing momentarily when I came to this chapter?!! Did you think that I was *playing* about not wanting to face this subject?! Do you know the amount of TRUTH it requires to AC-CEPT that you are not *only* insecure but also a *blatant* liar?!!! Come on, now. You have to walk WITH me in this self-realization!

<u>Lies are fueled by fear.</u>

Fear comes from the devil, the enemy. Fear is the opposite of faith. Mental habits formed due to past experiences **condition us** (inadvertently) to believe that if we tell the Truth (that someone may not want to hear), that it will hurt or upset the person that we are talking to –so it *probably* is better to <u>not</u> tell the Truth or at least not the ENTIRE Truth, so that they & us will walk away from this moment with (pretended) peace.

God told Joshua SEV-VER-RAL (several) times in Joshua Chapter 1 of the Holy Bible, that God *only* wanted Joshua to be strong & VERY courageous. It takes **absolute** courage to tell the Truth to someone or to people that very well may not *want* to *hear* what you have to say or may be disappointed in what Truth you offered. Especially more so, they may be disappointed when the Truth is in direct correlation with a decision or action made on *your* part.

We cannot forget the evil one, the devil –our enemy. It is & always will be his desire to influence us to <u>NOT</u> operate in our given, **God**-likeness & image

(Genesis 1-3). The devil aims to influence us *through* fear.

<u>When we are prone to tell the Truth, we are prone to act like God</u>. When we are prone to tell lies, cover up, deceive, withhold information or half-way tell what is accurate, we are agreeing to act like our enemy, the devil.

I am not sure about you, but this reality produces a very *awkward* feeling.

Do you know how many times I ½ way told the Truth, or left out portions of the Truth or completely LIED *altogether*, (alienating the Truth) due to fear of consequence?! *Pleaseeeeeee*...**do not act like** I am alone in this. (Side-eyed emoji) For we both know that THIS(!) is not Truth. The part that I truly do not like to accept, although I now **do** accept, is...anytime that I was willing to lie; it was because I was a *coward*.

Woooooooooooooooooooooooo! I **know**, *man*!!! It *does* hurt! But it is <u>still</u> TRUE! ANY time, you/we decided to lie, ½ way tell the Truth, diminish or omit information: it was simply because you/we were (at that moment) cowardly.

COWARD (n): is a person who *lacks* the courage to *do* or *endure* dangerous or *unpleasant* things; (adj): *excessively afraid* of danger or pain.

God said to me, "**People who are <u>insecure</u> are liars; because they don't have the *courage* to stand up for what is Truth...**" God said this to me MONTHS before I ever wrote this to you & *definitely* before I looked up the word 'coward'. God very specifically chose to use the word 'courage' in His statement. According to the definition, it is the *coward* who lacks courage. If you lack courage, you also lack confidence. **<u>If you lack confidence in telling the Truth</u>**, you are insecure.

INSECURITY (n): 1) uncertainty or anxiety about oneself; **<u>lack of confidence</u>**.

2) the state of being open to danger or threat; lack of protection.

People & **processes** have conditioned us (since birth) to be **programmed** to give the 'right' answer. The 'wrong' answer, *we may have learned*, possibly results in: over-criticism, disregard, *embarrassment, lengthy*-lecture, ostracism &/or undesired punishment. At this instant of spiritual development, we must now ask ourselves, " ***What is the*** *definition* ***of the 'right' & 'wrong' answers***?"

The appropriate Measuring Stick for what is right & wrong is: the Word of God.
–**Not:** trying to please people or trying to get to a certain position in life, nor trying to live a certain lifestyle, while maintaining a certain friend/network base.

Truth is right, depending on what <u>God</u> says in His Word.

You may be asking yourself, "So *now* what? I am just supposed to go telling everyone everything that I've ever lied about?" No...that is not what is being suggested here. The Holy Spirit is Alive & True. And I am not about to attempt to do *His* job. If we submit & commit ourselves to the Lord Christ Jesus, the **Holy Spirit** will instruct us in what He wants us to do, as He always does. The question is: **what will you (we) do from this moment forward?**

We can find peaceful resolve in making it our mission to live our lives in such a way that lying is not required; neither is it considered an option.

<u>Lying</u> (not telling the Truth) becomes the *defender* of **insecurity**.

Insecurity is the <u>lack</u> of confidence in standing up for what is True. We've lied because we were afraid of enduring unpleasant or possibly painful things. If we speak & act in a way that we are <u>not</u> afraid to repeat what we said & did, the bondage to fear is *then* broken. The **TRAP** of insecurity is *neutralized* when we make Truth our motive for thought, speech & conduct.

Making TRUTH our motive for thought, speech & conduct <u>will</u> pave the way for *disruption* of certain relationships & involvements. Some people only want to hear what *they* want to hear & only want to deal with you as long as you **do** what it is that **they want** *you* to do.

What will you tell that plutonic friend of yours the next time they want you to do something that you really do not want to do? You know that if you do not comply with their desire, that they will be upset with you, quite possibly give you the silent treatment & may even quit dealing with you altogether. It is **then** that you have to ask yourself, " *Were they really my friend at all?*"

Is a friend a friend based upon what you DO for them **or are they your friend because of the values & integrity that you possess** & live out???

With the people & processes that have conditioned us since birth to be programmed to give the 'right' answer, **this has taught us** (inadvertently) **to become accustomed to conditional-love.** "I have to do things *this* way or say things like *this* so that I won't be...*rejected.*"

We do not openly think or say this to ourselves, but our actions that do not align with Truth are indicative of this subconscious nature. We are afraid of the unpleasant thought that a relationship may end because we told the person Truth that they may not want to hear. We think that their *supposed* adoration for us may end; which we do not want. So we then create falsehoods & work to maintain a façade to uphold a (mis)representation of a caring relationship in our lives.

A major Truth that needs to be realized is that the *'right' or 'wrong'-answer* conditioning that we've become accustomed to, has subconsciously made us think that we have to 'do' things 'right' in order to receive love &/or acceptance. We do not want rejection; <u>rejection</u> is what we <u>fear</u> (both of the underlined are devices & **TRAP**s of the devil). So because we do not want to face the unpleasant *possibility* of rejection, we lie & *LIVE* LIES.

God, however, does not offer conditional love. God's Love is unconditional, never ending. *Love* is the very definition of WHO God IS. Any one that can **remove** their love for you from their heart never really loved you from the start. <u>I am not saying that</u>

people who actually love you won't ever leave you, because different circumstances produce different results! A battered wife is NOT expected to remain in a relationship with a man merely because she loves him. A devoted husband is not expected to stay in a relationship with a woman who is not faithful & has no desire to try to be. In these situations, the two parties can leave their significant other & still be fully loving of & *for* the person that was wronging them. The point: is that their Love for the other person did not negate the Love that they needed to have for a very important person, which is them*selves*.

We lie (or accept lies) because **we do not realize the value of who we are,** ***ourselves***. We think that if we tell Truth that may be undesired, that the party may walk away from us for good, wanting nothing more to do with us. But if this were to happen, their walking away does not mean that we are no longer deserving of Love! This <u>does not</u> mean that we should no longer Love ourselves.

If a person chose to walk away from us because of the hurt inflicted by the Truth that we offered IN God's Love, in essence they have that right to do so, since it is their choice. They have to take ownership for their decision(s). It is **your** decision to then, do as stated before: think, speak & act forwardly in such a manner, that verbally repeating your actions will not produce fear or insecurity within yourself because your motives for speech & conduct was based **on** Truth, not deceit nor intentional miscon-struing.

Regardless of who hurt you (originally & thereaf-ter), regardless how many times you've been used, abused, wronged, lied on, lied to, misunderstood, unappreciated, forgotten, unconsidered...YOU are WORTHY of LOVE. You do not have to DO THINGS to please people!!! This is True regardless of what positions people hold in your Life.

 You have to willingly obey God & His Word. God's Word is Truth. Your adherence to God's Ways will give you the **COURAGE** to be Truthful about your thoughts & actions. Obedience to God's statutes will make you bold in answering *for* your deeds. It is when we do things that are contrary to what is right (& we've learned that GOD's way is right), that fear is spiritually conceived & insecurity is birthed within us.

We must realize that in being a Truth-teller, it <u>IS</u> going to make some people *not* like you; it WILL make some people unpleased when you **don't fulfill** *their* expectations/desires. Should you tell the Truth without consideration of one's feelings? *–No.* We should always tell the Truth in a Loving way, *even* if it is done with firmness & sternness.

But do not expect to be Popular-Pat or Popular Patty. Other people have been conditioned to 'right' & 'wrong' answers as well. <u>And many more people create *their* relationships based upon people 'feeding' them what satisfies *their* created sense of what a 'friend' is & *does*.</u> But a REAL friend will tell the Truth even when it hurts you & hurts them.

Ultimately, we are not going to be able to BE these awesome Truth-tellers without constant prayer & cultivated relationships with God, Our Father. It is through constant communication **with** Him that we are built up in confidence to stand for what is REALLY right. And what is right is: *what God says.*

If people ditch us because we Lovingly told the
Truth & we are now active participants in LIVING
out Truth, (Truth to God, Truth to ourselves &
Truth to others), we must <u>let</u> them leave us. But
simultaneously, we HAVE TO KNOW that regardless of who stays or who chooses to go, WE are still
WORTHY of Love & we do not have to DO things
in order to receive Love!!! We are worth Love because we exist as God's beloved-creation! That's
what God says. Jesus died & rose again to prove it.
Nothing else matters...

We must first Love God. God will then teach us to
Love ourselves. **When we recognize we are valuable**
without **anyone's affirmation or commitment to us,**
we will <u>stop</u> people-pleasing!!!!! When we stop people-pleasing, we can *then* become advocates of
Truth. When we become willing advocates of
Truth, we annihilate insecurity.

Start anew from this moment forward! Yesterday
cannot be changed.
Today, Tomorrow & Beyond: Think, speak & act **in**
Truth so that you can be courageous. Then, we will
finally walk in TRUE security, breaking the bond-

ages of fear & lies <u>off</u> of our lives!!! Step WITH me OUT of Insecurity's **TRAP!**

Low Self-Concept

(the difference between Self-Concept & Self-Esteem)

All References for this Ingredient/Chapter 3, unless otherwise noted, will be used excerpts from the Psychology Book "Invitation to the Life Span" by Kathleen Stassen Berger

Did you know that there is a difference between self concept & self esteem? I didn't; until I was in the middle of a semester in my *Developmental Psychology* class. I love Psychology & have been a lover of it since being introduced to the subject in high school. Ever since its introduction to me, Psychology shaped & structured my mental processes.

So, this one night in class the teacher began to discuss the topic of *self-concept* vs. *self-esteem*. When hearing about a new psychological concept in class, my ears perked up! I hope you are ready for God's download using this psychological information!

Self-concept, according to the "Invitation to the Life Span", is: *a person's understanding of who he/she is, incorporating self-esteem, physical appearance, personality, & various personal traits, such as gender & size.*

Self-esteem, (same reference), is: *A person's evaluation of his/her own worth, either in specifics (e.g., intelligence, attractiveness) or in general.*

I have to say it again....Wooooooooooooooooooooooooooooo! So many thoughts flood my mind when reading these two definitions. Although they are psychological terms, God is going to show us how **spiritually** these terms are integral to understanding how we have been involved in so many demonic **TRAP**s. You *may* already have a clue...

According to the prior definitions, *self-concept* involves many things, **including** *self-esteem*. Since self-esteem is a foundational block in the *building of* one's self-concept, let us reflect on self-esteem a moment, then construct upward.

Self-esteem, psychologically, is summed up as having confidence in one's own aptitude. This sounds great on paper. But remember our task at hand; identifying the parts of the recipe for the devil's **TRAP**s in our lives. **Therefore we must delve into what issues** *produce* **low-self-esteem.**

As we discussed in Ingredient/Chapter 2: **_Insecurity_**, people are conditioned since birth about what is *perceived* as 'right' & 'wrong' answers. We have *also* been conditioned (either negatively or positively) concerning our self-esteem.

Our self-esteem is the cumulative evaluation of our **own** self-worth. But *this* self-worth is comprised **by what we've _heard the most_ about ourselves**...from *others*. Like my pastors Apostle Kelso & Apostle Jacqueline Clark often say, " *What you hear the most, you will believe the most. What you believe* *the most, you will do the most. And what you do the most is what you will manifest the most."*

It goes back to our childhood...sometimes, that ugly place that we want to just forget about. It may be <u>more</u> than one root of rejection that we have to face. If we are to walk in the Healing, the Fullness & the Wholeness of God, we must be willing to look back & identify where the thief, the devil, tricked us (Revelation 12:9) & what he stole from us.

On Page 198 of "<u>Invitation to the Life Span</u>", under the sub-title of ***Pride In Oneself,*** Berger states that *"some parents are routinely critical of their children. Such parents foster* [promote, create] *low-self esteem; the belief that "the self is fundamentally flawed" (Harter, 2006, p. 529).* It goes on further to say that: *"Extremely harsh criticism amounts to emotional abuse, causing children to develop a low estimate of their own competence that lasts life-long."*

This information is true, albeit concurrently sad. I know SOOOO many adults who do not think ANY thing positive about themselves. The only thing that they say is that they **"can't** do this" or they are **"not** good at doing that". Their personal belief in their inadequacies is so delusionally-strong & powerful that they believe that they cannot do things that they *have never attempted before*! The worse part of *this* is: that these **same** adults with these flawed, self-perceptions are conceiving & having children & are **smearing that same low mindset** on their off-spring (more than likely <u>unknowingly</u>).

It a disturbing, perpetual, self-generating, carnally-inherited, destructing force *intended* to annihilate God's image *in* His people. It is a generational attack from the devil that will not stop without enlisting God's Divine Help, alongside <u>our</u> determined, **personal** actions to insight change within *ourselves* & our seed, if applicable.

This issue is not one that is solely found in worldly people (people, who chose not to acknowledge, serve & obey Yahweh God); this issue is ever so prevalent among people who proclaim Christ Jesus as Lord. I know a woman who proclaims Christ Jesus to be her Lord & Savior. And due to not having any one EV-ER in her life tell her ANY thing positive about herself, her gifts (not even recognizing her gifts), her talents &/or abilities, <u>she doesn't believe any-thing positive about herself</u>. You can **actually wit-**

ness this woman doing a great job at something.
And she will never admit the same thing: that she
did or is *doing* a great job. She will excuse it off on
something else, other than herself. This woman is
very intelligent, good with money, is beautiful, is an
artist/sketcher, very resourceful, strong, a hard
worker...really a woman that **could do anything that
she set her mind to do**. But she is living a mediocre
existence because no one chose to verbally affirm
her **decades** ago. And because no one did, she thinks
her potential is not valid.

(!!!) **There does come a point, however, that WE**
(you, I, ALL OF US) **have to take responsibility for
our present & our future.** There is not one of us that
are responsible for the past that we were raised in.
Nor are we responsible for the *lack* of healthy child-
rearing/neglect that we *encountered*. But we **are**
responsible for the information that we have *now*;
the information that God has made available *to* us.

God said that we are to renew our minds & take on
the mind of Christ Jesus (Romans 12:2). **We are no
longer to be conformed to the mindset of the emotionally & spiritually, ignorant facilitators or un-**

participators of our childhood. Yes! This may sound brutal, but it is yet Truthful. We are <u>no longer to be conformed to the mindset of the emotionally & spiritually</u>, ignorant facilitators or <u>un</u>-participators of our childhood.

There are those who did not regard the intellect, emotions, mentality, sociality, physicality, or spirituality of the children that they bore. They only thought to *imitate what was shown to them* from the prior generation(s), **without thought** of *whether* the prior actions inflicted should be mimicked <u>or</u> forever renounced. They <u>did not</u> walk in *courage*; they did not *seek* from God what was Truth & they spewed falsehoods of insufficiency over yet *another* generation, misconstruing God's image & likeness within those same children.

<u>**How can we be believers of what the Word of God says that we can do, yet we don't believe that we can**</u> *<u>do</u>* **<u>anything</u>?** Do you see the embedded, internal lie?

This is why you can't receive a compliment! I was 25 years old before someone told me that I was 'beautiful'. And the person **saw** that I didn't believe it & they kept saying it until I cried. I cried because it seemed so hard to believe that it was true. (I thought)..."If it's true, *how come no one said it until now*???"

No! They did not validate you. No! They did not tell you that <u>you can do anything</u>! NO! They did not appreciate your gifts or recognize your talents. No! They did not support you in anything that you wanted to try to do that was NEW. Yes! They only treated you like a work-horse &/or a maid. Yes! The only attention you received was when they screamed, yelled at you, &/or beat you. Yes! They spent the majority of time with you, *actually ignoring* you. YES! They valued quietness over conversation with you. Yes! They operated in extreme denial that led you to be molested & raped & they did nothing about it afterward to try to protect or console you. Yes! They called you stupid. Yes! They called you fat! Yes! They said you were ugly. Yes! They said that no one would ever want you. Yes! They said that you would never be anyone, nor amount to anything good. BUT!!!!!!! Just because they said these things...<u>does not mean</u> that it was the Truth about you!!

Listen to God: "*It was not & it IS NOT the Truth about you. I made you in My Image & My Likeness. I AM none...of those things. And neither are you.*"

Once again, dear heart...the root/ingredient of rejection has produced a **TRAP**, fueled by the insecurity-ingredient, which leads to a **TRAP** *now secured* by low-self esteem.

When we operate in low-self esteem, we do not even want to get *out* of the **TRAP**. Someone can walk right up to us, remove the leaves, the bugs & the cob-webs, SHOW us the **TRAP**, & we shrug our shoulders & tell them that we can't get out, even when they are showing us HOW to get out.

Receiving & believing, ultimately AGREEING with the harsh criticisms or believing that neglect proves that we are less than adequate produces a terrible notion in our lives called: *victimhood*.

Victim is defined as: (n)-1) a person harmed, injured or killed as a result of a crime, accident, or other event or action OR, (n)-2) a person that is tricked or duped. Ummmmmmmm, *helloooo*??!!! I think that

we are going to go with door (definition) number
two!

That's the devil's entire M.O.: **trickery/deceit**.
Does the devil play fair? *–Um*, NO! And I am going
to tell you: if the devil decided to attack you in your
mind & your body, trying to destroy all self-esteem
in you since you were a CHILD...that means that
you are supposed to be a MIGHTY, POWERFUL,
ANOINTED individual <u>in</u> God. Why **else** would the
devil seek to alter your self-image ever since your
entire, first memories??!! The devil wanted you to
think & believe in the false-image of you that **he**
was projecting in your life. BUT THANKFULLY,
God allowed your path to come across the
knowledge of God's Truth (Jesus) and NOW you
have a Measuring Stick of what is right & what is
actually wrong.

I do not care if it **was** your Momma. Put up God's
requirements of what Love, humility, patience,
Wisdom & grace ARE, <u>beside</u> *her* depictions. If it
doesn't line up with God, her actions & speech &
thoughts are <u>not</u> OF God.
–It don't sound pretty, but it sho' is True (improper
English & all)! If it doesn't sound like God, nor talk

like God, nor ACT like God.....IT AIN'T
GODDDDD! Rehearse this in your spirit, until you
get it!

The devil doesn't care what person, or people or
places or things that he *uses* to try to destroy our
belief in OUR OWN God-likeness & self God-image
(Genesis 1:27). As long as <u>you</u> do not operate as God
in the earth AS God *instructed* you to, then the devil has free-course to run over **your** life & **you** permit
him to do the same to **your** seed through **your** deeds
or lack thereof.

We are called to walk in God's Kingdom-authority
HERE ON EARTH, NOTTTT in the 'sweet by &
by'...whatever a '*by & by*' is. God said that the
Kingdom of God is in **you** (Luke 17:20-21). But you
won't walk in God's son-ship (1 John 3:2) & king-
ship, as His priests on the earth (Revelation 1:6) until you **cancel** the suggested, *implanted* thoughts
<u>from the enemy</u>, by those who reared you. After you
cancel those suggested, implanted thoughts from
the enemy--by those who reared you, you THEN
have to choose to believe & be CONVINCED in the
Power of God that NOW is able to work through
YOU! (Ephesians 3:20). We can do all things

through Christ who strengthens us! (Philippians 4:13)

The question is: do we *want* to be strengthened or do we want to remain **TRAP**ped sheep looking for someone to lick our wounds & feel sorry for us 70 years after the inflicted & imposed hurt? *At what hour*, will you decide that God is Sovereign & that what He says **is** what goes for YOUR Life? When are you going to realize & ACCEPT that Christ Jesus gave His Blood as **The** Sacrifice so that you could be reconciled BACK to God & *re*-receive your rightful position as a joint-heir *with* Christ Jesus (Romans 8:17)? You, being a joint-heir with Christ Jesus means: that you are now eligible to receive the same backing of Power *from* God *Himself* in your Life.

The lack of initiated support & lack of proper direction from those who knew **nothing** of the purpose or role of raising children does not mean that YOU continue (in your adulthood) to attach yourself to *those* beliefs of the ignorantly un-informed. Your role *now* is to discover WHO God says *you* are, WHAT God says your purpose is & HOW you are to carry out His Will in the earth.

<u>In this last day that we are *now* in,</u> victimhood is no <u>longer popular.</u>

–And anyone that is tolerating the victim-mindset, is sitting in the dusty-spiritual **TRAP** *with* you. Let's decide to get out of the **TRAP** of low-self esteem *today*; God *Himself* is holding the **TRAP** open. Jesus died & rose again, so that you may be freed from the enemy: free in Life, free in your mind, free in your spirit, free in your soul & free in your body. Choose to get up and get OUT of low-level thinking...now!

Wow! I know that was a lot that God just deposited into us. And amazingly we only discussed one of the two topics of this 3rd ingredient/chapter. Let us continue forward. The second subject is: Self-Concept.

Self-concept, according to the "Invitation to the Life Span", is: *a person's understanding of who he/she is, **incorporating self-esteem,** physical appearance, personality, & various personal traits, such as gender & size.*

Self-esteem is a *part* of your self-concept.

An improper assessment of your own worth (insuffi-cient self-esteem), **will cause your** *understanding* **of WHO YOU ACTUALLY ARE** (your self-concept) **to be inadequate.** If your self-esteem is off, then it's seems obvious that your self-concept will be off.

My ears perked up in Psychology class when these two topics were mentioned; primarily because I con-sidered self-concept & self-esteem to be one & the same. But *if* self-concept is made up **of** self-esteem (among other things), then self-concept has to be a **more** *detailed* concern.

According to the definition of *self-concept* that we read prior, it is the ***understanding*** of who you are. This **understanding** is comprised of *your* thoughts concerning: your self-esteem, your physical appear-ance, your personality, & other personal traits, in-cluding your gender & size.

The Holy Bible (Kings James Version) says in Prov-erbs 4:7 that "Wisdom is the principle thing: and with all thy getting, get **understanding**." I think that it's very noteworthy that when it comes to self-concept, it primarily deals with **your understanding** of who you *actually* are.

(!!!)<u>Who can tell creation what it (rightfully) is, except the One Who is the Creator?</u> (!!!) Our understanding of who we are comes from what **God** says we are & what God says we are not.

If you've **believed** the negative lies that were told to you since childhood <u>or</u> if no one said anything at all to you about who you were, leaving you to assume negative thoughts that you believed were validated by the lack of involvement &/or lack of concern from those who reared you, your understanding of who God says you are will be very, very skewed.

<u>Wisdom</u> is the principle thing. **Wisdom is primary**. It is the most important concern. *Obviously*, poor child rearing is *not accomplished* by those possessing wisdom. Because we cannot change our childhoods, we must act upon what we are <u>now</u> able to modify. Wisdom is the principle thing & with all

the getting that we attempt in Life, wisdom is the thing that we must seek to obtain *first*. –We must NOW seek the wisdom that tells us who we are, according to God's Word.

If you go by the world's suggestions & standards concerning your physical appearance, your personality, & other personal traits, including your gender & size, more than likely you are going to be MORE messed up NOW than you were as a child. The world's suggestions through audio & visual airwaves, as well as social media & magazines, ALL will tell you that you are not good enough when it comes to these specific areas of yourself.

Why else are there now thousands of people who are walking around in internal distress, paying lump sums of money, willing to go into debt, only to look like stretched, plumped, neo-mannequin-people? There are TV shows galore that propose that unless you are nasty in attitude <u>&</u> in appearance (sexually-tactless) that you aren't worthy of attention. And now, there are people who are choosing to live out their *personal* lusts, claiming their desires to be 'natural'....

–although **<u>completely contrary</u>** to what God's Word

says. (James 1:14 says that... "Everyone is tempted when he drawn away by his OWN lust & enticed...")

Everything about the world tells you to "do what thy wilt" (an <u>irrefutably</u>, demonic term/statute) & to forget & alienate any sort of reverence for Yahweh God, the Great I AM & what it is that **His** Word states. The world was once subtly trying to convince people that a little of 'this' won't hurt. **Now the world & its idols** (all people exalting themselves above God) **are saying**: '*to leave Yahweh, the only Wise God, in order to get what you* **want!** *Degradate yourself & drink this blood, offer the sacrifice & you'll be famous & rich. You only live once. YOLO, everybody!*'

The worldly-accepted projection *now* is to quit believing in the Only-Wise God, altogether. ___*What afterlife*___, when you've *chosen* to believe in nothing but satisfying yourself? Seeking the world for what 'everybody' says you *should* be doing & for what is 'commonly' acceptable <u>IS not</u> wise. It is **very** foolish.

In order to get a proper perception of your physical appearance, your personality, & other personal traits, *including* your gender & size, you <u>must first</u> <u>discover</u> what God's Word says.

If you are overweight, don't have the hair or the hair length or hair type that you'd like, if you don't think you are funny or think that you aren't serious enough, even IF you wish that you were a different gender (uh-oh! She **talked** about it!), you are STILL made in God's image. God made you the way that you...ARE. Out of all the personal traits that were mentioned earlier, the only one that you really have extreme, personal control over would be your weight. If you are overweight, it is going to take due diligence to combat that physical concern. It *will* be hard work. But you should do it because you **love yourself** & want to be the best, healthy *version* of yourself, NOT try to lose weight because you *want* love or hope to be accepted.

NOW...when it comes to this gender concern, I am going to put it this way. Years ago, WAYYYYYYYYYYYYY before this new rebellious, revolution of "do what thy wilt" –sexually, (YES! I said it!), I had a conversation with someone that was decades older than me. I asked them if they thought that people were 'born' homosexual or lesbian. They asked me what I thought. And I told them that ultimately, it wasn't something that I could personally prove, but that I was aware of 1 particular kid that always 'acted' like the opposite sex, even when we all were very, very young. Considering **this** information, I asked the person what *they* thought.

After thinking for a considerable amount of time, the person said something that I regarded as VERY profound. They said that they themselves could not prove whether or not someone was born with an attraction to the same sex or not. <u>But they do know that God's Word clearly states</u> that we are all tempted & enticed according to our OWN, *personal* lusts (James 1:14). That means that what *you* lust for, will not necessarily be the thing that I lust for.

Lust can be defined as: having a self-absorbed (if not checked, over-whelming) **desire for an <u>object</u>, <u>person</u> or <u>experience</u>**. Participating in lust means that we have placed the object of our craving **above** all things in our lives. The most particular concern is that we placed our lust & the *fulfillment* of our lust <u>OVER</u> the principles that God dictates in His Word!!! **The Truth: is that we should not reveren-**

tially place <u>any</u>-thing over God. Our desires are included in this.

We are to cast down (**deliberately** <u>not</u> **meditate on**) <u>every</u> vain imagination & mentally cast down every high thing that exalts itself AGAINST the knowledge of God! WE are to *MAKE* our thoughts obey Christ Jesus (2 Corinthians 10:5).

Using meditation to live out lustful fantasies **in** our imagination, *whatever lustful thought(s) it might be*, opens the door to carnality (...which is what the devil is **waiting** on *daily*). Meditating on lustful thoughts (2 seconds or longer) self-surrenders *you* to bondage to these thoughts, eventually causing you to want to **act** out what you've mentally entertained. I am actually speaking from **personal** experience concerning lustful thoughts towards the same sex. I have ONLY seen & experienced personal victory because of adamant adherence to 2 Corinthians 10:5. **It is** a fight, but belief **in** & submission **to** God's Word will give you <u>actual</u> Strength in moments of temptation & weakness.

I really could go further, but it is **not** the intention to harp on one facet of turmoil *within* the self-concept. It is only **in** <u>possessing belief that God's</u>

Word <u>**is** the Truth</u> & **The** Final Authority in our lives <u>that we will find the Power</u> to walk **triumphantly** concerning improper perceptions & internal conflict within our self-concept.

As already clearly shown, this book that you are now reading is based upon belief in God's Holy Word.

If you do not want help or change or guidance according to what God's Word states, I am not sure why you are reading *this* material.

Attacking our self-esteem &, in due course, our self-concept is the devil's motive to change your AWARENESS concerning your **God**-like image (Genesis 1:27). If you do not know NOR **understand** WHO you are as a child of God, if you do not know your rights as a citizen within God's Kingdom, you will <u>not</u> walk in God's Authority. You will not operate as a king under King Jesus, decreeing & declaring (Romans 4:17) & binding & loosing (Matthew 18:18) what **shall** be *according* to what God's Will is.

Choosing to cling to low-self esteem destroys potential for *suitable* self-concept. It is the devil who
comes to steal, kill & destroy us & things connected
to us (John 10:10). From this day forward, if you
consciously choose to facilitate (assist) & foster (cul-
tivate) low-level thinking **within** *yourself, knowing*
these thoughts are **completely** contrary to God's
thoughts (Jeremiah 29:11), you must ask *yourself,*
"Whose side am I really on: God's side or the devil's
side?"

If you are truly on God's side, this will **require** you
to think/say the things about *yourself* that **God** says
about you in His Word. Doing & believing God's
Word, will REVITALIZE your self-esteem, renew
your self-concept & pull you out of yet another spiritually-binding **TRAP**. It's time to think & believe
higher thoughts about yourself (like God does)...so
that we can move on to a *better* us...in *this* Life.

INGREDIENT FOUR

Abandonment

(which...is different from Rejection: mentally, emotionally, physically, & spiritually)

Hold *on*, dear one!

I know that this book & what God is saying is causing us to look at our*selves* & forcing us to take responsibility in ways that we may not have originally deemed necessary. And if you are like me, it may feel uncomfortable. But it is for our good! (Romans 8:28) But God needs us to dig & go deep(er) – scooping & scraping out all remnants of the rusty residue that has been tainting our spirits for **so** long. As we move further*, together*..............

What is another ingredient in the devil's (*our enemy*) recipe for tempting, trying, tricky **TRAP**s?..............................*Abandonment.*

Abandon (v): is defined as: 1) give up completely (a course of action, a practice, or a way of thinking); 2) cease to support or look after someone; to desert.

I wonder if you are like me; I asked within myself, "What is the **difference** between rejection & abandonment, *God?* They 'seem' to be the same..." But remember as stated earlier: it's *always best to research what <u>may</u> even appear simple,* because our understanding may be incomplete in *some* manner.

In Ingredient/Chapter 1, we reviewed that ***Rejection*** is (the root word 'reject' is defined as,) one that has been discarded or refused.

In seeking God for the difference between these two concepts, God said (<u>not</u> verbatim) that ***abandoning*** someone was *more severe* than ***rejecting*** someone. <u>Contemplating on this thought,</u> it *can* be under<u>stood why</u>. When someone or something is rejected, in essence, the *act of rejecting* indicates that the ***as-***

sessor found the subject matter to NOT be 'up-to-par', according to the guidelines that the assessor *personally* regards as pertinent. We are not saying that any said guidelines are right or wrong; we are currently looking at the concept of rejection from a *completely,* **objective** *standpoint.*

Abandonment, on the other hand, **denotes alienation.** This is a very POWERFUL, Rhema (downloaded) statement straight from The Holy Spirit. **Abandonment denotes alienation.** *Alienation* (n): is the state or experience of being isolated or <u>detached</u> from a person, group or activity to which one **SHOULD** belong or in which one **SHOULD** be involved.

In *rejection,* you may have been **deceived** *into a belief* or you merely *chose* to believe in a direction-less delusion that rendered you being discarded. In *abandonment* (however), you were living your life <u>**rightfully**</u> thinking that you were involved in a relationship (professional, ma-/paternal, platonic, &/or personal), *expecting* that responsibility & accountability would be the foundational composition...& for <u>one</u> reason or another, **you were abruptly deserted.**

Again...

Abandon (v): is defined as: 1) give up completely (a course of action, a practice, or a way of thinking); 2) cease to support or look after someone; to desert.

Abandonment is a sharp **TRAP** laden with millions of finger-length, needle-like spikes. The **TRAP** itself is <u>small</u>, only large enough to confine the devil's main, *coveted* target: our heart.

How many times have we pushed, pulled, cried, begged, pleaded, prodded, tried, revised, recreated, simplified, copied, over-indulged, were silent, screamed, prayed, hoped, dreamed, gave up, gave in, jumped 'hoops', what-have you...INTENTIONALLY...for another human being...wanting to do all that you could to '**make**' things work...*ONLYYYYY*....to have them leave you or discount you without explanation or they could have left you with a **vague** explanation that only resulted in confusion for *you*. They could have left you in Life or they could have left you by dying or left by '*choosing*' death. They could have 'gone' to the store 29 years ago & **still** haven't returned. They could have 'been' with your sibling or your baby-sitter (had sex) while you were away (or just a *room* away) & then decided to give you up completely (you...as their original 'vision').

<u>Or</u>, you could have come home & all of your loved one's possessions were gone, as if a subjective thief robbed your home, considering *your* things as sacred in the heist. You could have found out 'accidently' that your loved one that you've been 'involved' with, had someone *else* **all along** (or some other ELSES –improper English & all) & that the person *you* were 'involved with' is in the process of working towards marriage –with someone *else...* <u>WHILE</u> *being*...with *you...*

You could have been a baby/child/young adult left in an unsafe environment <u>or</u> left at the hospital, or left with family, friends or strangers –**not adopted** (which is *generally* a loving choice on both sides), but just *left*. –<u>Given up on</u>, *completely discarded*; support system ceased; deserted.

The thing that God keeps saying to me (right now) concerning these things (& even situations not men-

tioned), in relation to being abandoned is this:
"Where there is no vision, the people perish..."
(Proverbs 29:18).

HOW?   HOW is THIS relational?
A vision is beyond mere physical sight. A vision (as
in a vision-statement) is spiritual fore-sight. It's a
self-standardized, personally-initiated & implemented code of morals, guidelines & goals **projected
towards** & **based on** God's Purpose & Will **for** the
relative participants in the *said* vision.

In any & all circumstances, if God's Will & Word <u>is
not</u> sought in how one will make *their* decisions, in
how they will *conduct* themselves, in WHO they will
attach <u>&</u> connect themselves to mentally, emotionally, physically, financially, socially, &/or spiritually,
the partakers in the vision will <u>**experience**</u> *eventual*
<u>**abandonment**</u>.

Please let the prior statement sink into your spirit...
In any & all circumstances, if God's Will & Word <u>is
not</u> sought in how one will construct their decisions
concerning connections, **at least one of the partakers
of the vision will experience** *eventual* **abandonment**
(whether or not the vision is written <u>or</u> declared).
You may live 20 years physically with someone, but

spiritually they have left you <u>in</u> solitude with zero regard.

Being abandoned can cause **us** to abandon God, intentionally or inadvertently. Either way, abandoning the ways & the cause of our King Jesus is imperceptive (simple-minded). The eventual end of <u>our</u> chosen way (decisions ***outside*** of God's Counsel) contains *inevitable* sadness & heartbreak. **Taking current charge over our decisions** (now), **we must realize that we have to** <u>include</u> **God in our decisions & ask for Wisdom** (James 1:5) BEFORE **forming alliances & relationships** (platonic, professional & monogamous)!

Hosea 4:6 says, "...My people are destroyed from the **lack** of knowledge. Because you have rejected knowledge, I also reject you as My priests [ministers/teachers/intercessors]; because you have ignored the law of your God, I will also ignore your children..." (*New International Version*)

God is the Great I AM. He is Almighty & *completely* able to be what it is that we *need* Him to be, in ANY given situation. However, when we **abandon** His ways for our own, He respects our freedom of choice & allows us to have our own, *rebellious* way. The unfortunate thing is that in **not** seeking God, we create a generational curse. **God-less decisions** (decisions based SOLELY on what YOU want or what YOU think) cause your children & *every generation afterward* to be **ignored** by God.

Do not get it confused. God rains on the just & the unjust (Matthew 5:45). But you and your seed can not live from a place of *sacred expectation* of God to have your back when you have decided to *turn your back* on seeking God for proper direction OF your way(s). His Word declares you are entitled to live in expectation of God's protection AND provision when you do things *His* Way. Importantly, please note: the generational curse(s) will not stop until someone in the lineage decides that as for themselves & *their* family/household, they are going to choose to do things God's way! (Joshua 24:15)

Another weighty point to acknowledge concerning abandonment is found in the definition of the word alienation. Remember alienation *stems from* abandonment.

Alienation (n): is the state or experience of being isolated or detached from a person, group or activity to which one *should* belong or in which one *should* be involved.

The reflective thought to take note of, is that the major hurt encompasses the idea that the subject matter that abandoned you, is someone that you SHOULD belong to or SHOULD be involved *with*.

The word 'should' denotes a sense of *entitlement.* **This is where the internal injury stems from!** This 'thing' SHOULD **not** have happened. 'Should' deals with expectancy. When we SHOULD belong to something, someone, or to a cause (because of a TWO-WAY acknowledgement AND agreement; a covenant; an understanding) and WE are erroneously relinquished & renounced by the *other* party *without* concern OR prior notice, that *heart-sized* **TRAP** is set to be *sprung* by the seeds of: bitterness, unforgiveness, anger, fear, pride & doubt being grown & rooted IN YOUR HEART, *within* the **TRAP**.

You see, THIS **TRAP** is *sneaky*. This **TRAP** does not SNAP shut. It lays wide open covered by debris, attempting to be unrecognizable. This **TRAP**, however, gets woven like an Indian 'dream-catcher'. Bitterness, unforgiveness, anger, fear, pride & doubt are the painful threads that weave & bob to sew the teeth of the **TRAP** shut (in & through the heart). The reason why this **TRAP** is tricky is because bitterness, unforgiveness, anger, fear, pride & doubt mask themselves as devices of one word: ***protection***.

You *know* that this is true!!!
.....“I'll NEVER trust them again!” “I'll never give my heart to anyone *else* like that **again!**” “That was the last time.” “I'm *done* with love.” “I don't trust people.” “I won't trust people.” “I will depend on myself only.” “I don't *let* people get close to me.” ...is what we've said.

Because of abandonment, we attempt to protect *ourselves*. We build walls around our *hearts*. If that person, place or thing did this to me, if *they* abandoned & left me out here on my own & they were '**supposed**' to be the one(s) that cared about **our agreed covenant**, then HOW am I supposed to trust ANY one else ever again???!!!!!!

Honestly, this is a very, **valid** question.

I am not going to sit here & act like I have it all together in this area. Actually, it has been quite the
opposite. You can ask anyone that has any (real)
clue as to *how* I think (...some people *think* they
know you & they **really** do not): I am the absolute
last person to trust someone. (HARD! –for those
who know me...) For *re-al*!

Life has shown me tooooooo many instances, too
many repeat episodes to where it's getting easier to
(spiritually) **detect** devilish motives & outcomes
(even in those who are declared, prophesying saints
running around God's church). BUT: I am led to
say, that we must acknowledge God in ALL our
ways & HE will DIRECT our paths (Proverbs 3:4-
6).

This is one comforting Truth that I can offer you:
God WILL lead you into ALL Truth through and
by His HOLY SPIRIT (John 16:13)!!! I am **telling**
YOUUUUUUUUUUUUU! This is for REAL!

I prayed to God a long time ago, "God, please **always**
show me the **TRUE** hearts of men (people). Please
God, **always** let me know, *without doubt*, whose
heart is *REALLY* for me & whose heart is REALLY

against me." EV-ER since, I prayed <u>that</u> prayer, God does *precisely* this, with *accuracy*! He has not ceased in this area one moment! God shows me in **various**, specific ways, who is *really* for me & who is against me *secretly* in their heart(s), minds & actions. *Now,* (healthily) I can go from not trusting *anyone*...to being *cautious* of whom the Holy Spirit gives me an internal 'check' about.

WE must remember that the devil's (our enemy) **foremost <u>coveted target</u> is OUR hearts.** Rejection is the primer & platform for low-self-esteem & low-self-concept. Abandonment is the glossy sealant falsely validating the original seeds of rejection. The heart is the <u>focal</u> point of the devil's attack(s). And the reason that this is, is due to the fact that the heart is where things are birthed.

Your mind is the receiver of information. <u>It is only when your **heart** is connected to a thought that conception to a belief is formed within your spirit & psyche.</u>

The God-likeness & God-image <u>within</u> you is what the devil is <u>after</u> because that is where your <u>power & authority</u> (in God—*OVER* the devil) **resides** (Genesis 1:27). If you have been conditioned to believe that you are not worth proper Love (because of rejection) & **then, you get abandoned** by someone that said that they 'would *be* there for you', your heart goes on 'lock-down' mode.

You shut down & shut off your Love receptacles. This may not seem like a big deal, but it really is. Without faith it is impossible to please God (Hebrews 11:6). "What are you talking about, **man**?! I thought that you were talking about LOVE!" I AM, dear one. I AM.

In Galatians 5:6 (Amplified Version), it says in summary that **faith** is activated & energized & expressed & working THROUGH Love. This means that faith cannot be in actual operation in your Life if you do not have Love operating in your heart.

How is THIS so?
God Himself, is Love. 1 John 4:8 says that whoever does not Love, does not know God, because God is Love. Do you see the spiritual equation(s) formulated? **GOD=Love**. *Faith is worked by Love, which equals* = Faith is worked by God.

According to Genesis 1:27, we are made in God's image & likeness, which means: **We=Love**. If we do

not Love, we have <u>no true God-like faith</u> in operation in our Lives, *meaning* **we do not have God's**
Power in operation in our Lives.

If we have no (God-like) faith, we are not pleasing
God. If we are not pleasing God, then that means
that we are not reflecting/resembling God's image,
but we are taking on the image of the Love-
imposter, the devil. If we do not Love, we are not
walking in our instituted God-likeness & God-
image.

From the beginning of time, the God-likeness & the
God-image *within* **man-kind is what the enemy, the**
devil, has been after! Remember, it is <u>in</u> your God-
likeness & <u>in</u> your reflective God-image that you
have POWER <u>OVER</u> the devil, spiritually & naturally!

Since the devil has no power over you, his only option is the spirit of INFLUENCE. The devil uses
situations & circumstances to try to SWAY your
thoughts (which are the entry way to the heart) to
come OUTSIDE of the confines & *safety* of what
God's Word says is True about you & your Life.
When you think & believe *contrary* to what God's
Word says, your God-likeness & God-image is dis-

torted & cloudy. Your **God**-given power is temporarily suspended/stunted, <u>because **your** lack of faith
blocks the Power</u>, because your Love receptor is in
the mode of 'OFF'.

Do you see why rejection & more so *abandonment*
are **TRAPs**?

<u>The question that the devil will always ask</u> about
<u>every born individual on the face of this planet is
this</u>: "*how* can I deter, discourage & dissuade this
person from the course of God?" Perpetual rejection
reinforced by abandonment is the ultimate **TRAP** to
turn your heart into stone. (**Trust** me; I *know.*) A
cold, faithless heart that does not believe in people
(or God's Way) is a deceptive, protective measure
intended to keep **you** bound & locked in a *God-less*
situation with *no self-initiated-Power* to get out.
BUT!!! You CAN get out of the **TRAP** of abandonment!!! (Hallelujah!)

I **KNOW** it hurt! I know that it still *does* hurt. I
know they lied. They cheated you &/or cheated *on*
you. They walked away from you. They lived their
lives as if you didn't exist or as if your feelings
didn't matter. They didn't think about what they

were leaving you *to*. They don't know the hell that you encountered due to their covenant-withdrawal. **I know that people that <u>you</u> respect act like "you should be *over* it by now"**. I know that people act like "you *should have* **known** better...". I know that you want to quit believing in people & keep a distance from others within your heart. But dear one, this is not God's way.

I am certified to discuss this. I've been hurt & rejected from the beginning. Factually speaking, rejected & abandoned by my father. 14 years later rejected & abandoned by my mother (due to unhealthy relationship & lack of understanding). –Led through despair to life in the street, which is **laced** with additional rejection & deception. Eventual, participation in a 5+ year, abusive relationship, forged with lies & unknown deceit. All of this left me thinking that I could trust no one & that the only one that would have my back is me & *hopefully* God.

But this mindset kept me bound.
Yes. It felt good not having to worry about letting people in, nor being concerned with forgiveness or trust. But I had neither power nor *any* peace to tru-

ly be an over-comer in any situation. I was in a self-made prison. And THIS is contrary to my (our) God-like Purpose in the earth.

It is when we Love, in *spite* of, that we are *most* like God! (WOW!) God gave the world Jesus, to die for the sins of all of mankind, even when WE cared nothing about Him or even believed that He did so.

God created us to reign in this earth, NOW (Revelation 5:10). But we can't have victory in our situations until we get a new perspective, a new heart. We <u>have</u> to reign over evil that *tries* to infiltrate our hearts. This is something that we will have to do <u>over & over again</u>, successfully achievable with God's help.

God said that He will give us a new heart & put a new spirit within us. God said that He will take out our stony, hard heart & give us a heart that is pliable & *once again* tender (Ezekiel 36:26). This is God's image: *tender-heartedness.*

It is not God's will that any should perish, nor be separated from God. This is the ENTIRE reason why God put Himself in a Human body, via <u>Holy</u> Conception through His Holy Spirit, to be born into the world, so that He could offer Himself as a Holy Sacrifice. –To be the Atonement for the sins of all. Only *extreme* Love, *extreme* concern, & *extreme* compassion would do that! Especially considering that the majority of the world is *rejecting* God's Sacrifice (Jesus) & abandoning God's Love.

Abandonment can become a generational curse. Abandonment is <u>not limited</u> to physical desertion. Abandonment is a **TRAP** to cause improper self-image to set in. **Abandonment does not dictate your worth.**

Abandonment is an opportunity to draw *closer to* God & God promises to come closer to you (James 4:8). Abandonment can be **conquered** through **proper** God-like perception.

Abandonment has to do with LACK of vision within the *withdrawer*!!!!!!!!!!!!!!

Connect **only** with people whose visions are God-*inspired* & God-*purposed* (**for** *you*!). Make sure that you *yourself* are God-inspired & God-purposed. <u>Know</u>

that you are **worth** Love & that you are called to **BE LOVE** in spite of circumstances. Being Love does not require accepting abuse or neglect. Being Love does not require believing lies, nor succumbing to lustful, peer pressure. Being Love does not require us being played, used, or dangled. Hold up **the God-standard**. Be Love & Love from afar, if necessary.

People's lack of Love doesn't mean that you should shut off *your* Love receptacles. Love is your connection to God & His Ways. Love is *how* you release God from within **you**. Love is how you work your faith & gain access to God's Power that Jesus died & resurrected for you to have. God is Love & Love is WHO you ARE!

Abandonment is a **TRAP** to *harden* your heart. When your heart hardens, your image changes from God's image to the devil's image. This morphed change is the lie that the devil wants you to believe in: that this is *now* **who** you are. This is why the **TRAP** of abandonment is tricky. Loose & let go of the devil's *suggestive* thoughts & ways.

Love exists within you regardless of the actions of others. **BE, Love**.

Change your course by changing your mind. Doing so, will *activate* God's Power within you & you will walk <u>out of</u> abandonment *affected*, but alive. **Clinging to God**, you'll be healed in your spirit *with newness* & set free.

Let's leave abandonment's **TRAP**...together. *You ready?* On the count of 3: 1...2...3eeeee!

INGREDIENT FIVE

Spiritually, **fear** is a binding, *restrictive* agent. Remember: this book is all about the components that the devil uses in his recipe(s) for **TRAPs** in our lives. **TRAPs** are demonic <u>situations intended to keep us in mental, spiritual & emotional lock-down.</u> FEAR is the most *intricate* component regarding **TRAPs**. FEAR is the **TRAP** that we will *forever* have to <u>denounce</u> in order to walk in the authority of Power, with our given, God-likeness.

<u>GOD</u>, our Creator, (the One *scientists* like to ignore & renounce, even though God MADE→ science) The **Great I AM**, Yahweh, Jehovah God, The Ancient of Days, the

Lord Christ Jesus, Yoshua *Himself,* via His Holy Spirit, **created** the human body to have *autonomic* (subconscious) & *systemic* reflexes in *response* to fear in given situations. Your internal reaction(s) will trigger you to properly respond so that *survival* will be the goal/desired outcome.

NOTE: This has nothing to do with *evolution* (which is a man-made theory to appease self-righteousness). Fear did not 'get birthed' inside of us spontaneously so that we wouldn't get eaten by a saber-tooth tiger after our tad-pole tails fell off. (Prior statement was completely sarcastic. God did not create us with any former, earthly encasement; only the human body, as it is currently.)

God *allowed* the fear-trigger response within us so that we can have a chance to avoid eminent peril by *suitably* **taking action**. Avoiding hazard is **how** we maintain existence. Chemically, the fear response is primarily *autonomic.* It isn't something that you intentionally trigger inside of yourself. Its prompted, innate response is a God-given, *survival* tactic. Fear is activated when your brain senses danger, harm &/or trouble, **or** when your *brain* ***anticipates*** danger, harm &/or trouble.

WHEN IT COMES TO THE DEVIL...

We must focus on the **anticipation** of fear. This is why spiritually, fear is a binding agent; this is why fear is not beneficial. When we fear just TO fear, we have taken on a mindset that is not of God. Any mindset that is not of God is of the devil. There is no uncertainty about this.

Anticipate – (v.) means: regard as *probable*; expect or predict; look forward to; guess or be aware of (what will happen) & take action in order to be *prepared.*

The devil, the enemy of man, wants us to live with a fearful mindset even when there is **no actual** endangerment to confront (Proverbs 28:1). The devil is a great illusionist, a master of deceit & a manipulative-*mental* influence. <u>Living in fearful expectation</u>

greatly *controls* & *lowers* your self-esteem & your self-concept.

You are called to operate with God's Power **in the earth.** (Psalm 82:6) This is why Jesus died & was resurrected by the Holy Spirit! Jesus offered His Blood to Father God so that YOU & I can have a *renewed* covenant with God, **which entitles us to have access to God's Power!!!** Believing in the work of Jesus on the cross of Calvary & accepting His Sacrifice for mankind, makes us now joint heirs **with** Christ Jesus (Romans 8:17). Walking in fearful anticipation, you cannot operate in the Power of God. THIS...is why the devil would always want you to LIVE in the **TRAP** of FEAR.

The anticipation (or should we say, the **self-creation**) of fear *discourages* action. It is the thoughts that we mediate on & *entertain* that *we* permit to influence our decisions, which then influences our actions. *Self-created fear?* Yes. –When thoughts 'told' you that you *should* be afraid; not because of *actuality*, but because of a mere *thought* & *assuming* that the thought is fact.

For example: *public speaking* (supposedly the #1 fear for humans after the fear of death). Why do humans

fear public speaking? It is because of the thoughts!!!
What thoughts? The thoughts that **you** have about
what **you** think *others* may think!!! ↓

" *What if I sound stupid?* (Low-self worth) *What if
they don't like me?* (Low-self concept) *I'm so nervous.
What if I start stuttering? What if I forget the subject matter? The last time, the people's faces looked
totally disinterested. I hate hearing myself speak.
They probably will too...*"

NONE of these thoughts (↑) were validated by any
Truth.

Your *decided* mental connection to these thoughts
influenced your body to **now** respond to a fear that is
not authentic. You do not **know** why the people's
faces looked like they did when you last spoke. They
could have gotten into an argument before attend-
ing your presentation. They *could* have received a
negative health report. They *could* be behind in
their mortgage & afraid them*selves*. They *could*
have had intense, intestinal gas OR about to run
OUT of gas in their vehicle!!! Faces do not 'tell' it
all.

Just like you can't judge a book by its cover, you cannot judge the donner (the wear-er...) by the face. Allowing fearful *thoughts* to **convert** to *beliefs* is a MISTAKE & is a step on a demonic-merry-go-round **intended** to be a negative blue-print for your very Life.

–Ritualistically going round & round, **running from ideas that** *aren't* **confirmed or correct.**

These days, the devil is trying to make people think that fear is *nonchalant*, child's play. *Sure*...the movie & entertainment industry are capitalizing on **Fear**--offering all of these 'paranormal' & demonic activities for viewing so that *darkness* can have entrance into the eye-gates of unaware people (Matthew 6:22). And while great spiritual desensitization has occurred widespread to where fear is a now a *desired* emotion, people have been deceived into having an *admiration* of the powers of wickedness. All in all, **unwarranted**, **unnecessary** fear is of the enemy, the devil. This same fear internalized, is a prison –a self made cage, also known as a **TRAP**.

Let us reflect & remember what we discussed in Ingredient/Chapter 2: *Insecurity*. God said, "**People**

who are insecure are liars; because they don't have
the courage to stand up for what is Truth..." The key
point to focus on in God's revelatory statement is
that liars & those who operate in insecurity *really*
operate IN *fear*. <u>Fear is their mode of operation.</u>
The lack of courage can be equated with fear. What
does *this* fear have to do with *media-portrayed* fear?

Subtle, sneaky, & sly are the traits of our adversary,
the devil. <u>The devil's aim is *always* to make you
think that there is nothing wrong with something
that is **actually** wrong.</u>

> *"What's the big deal about a movie with people
> playing demonic games & participating in demonic
> practices? People think that evil spirits, witchcraft
> & magic are 'cool' these days. What's the big deal
> about not standing up for what is Truth? People
> think what they **want** to think. Do, **you!** Everyone is
> doing 'it'. Why would I want to ostracize myself?
> Nobody upholds 'that' standard anymore. Times
> have changed. You have to 'go with the flow'. You
> are just 'old-fashioned'...."*

In whatever form it comes, fear (in your heart) is
intended (by the devil) to influence you to **not** act in

some way, shape or form. Media-produced fear is relational to the point being made because the devil, the enemy of man, is trying to make people so *desensitized* that they aren't attentive or <u>sensitive</u> (**spiritually**) enough to *detect* when fear is binding them in their **own** lives!!! The devil is trying to get people <u>accustomed</u> to fear...so that there will not be a *realization or revelation* of the <u>*need*</u> to be liberated when the devil comes with his spiritual nooses.

Desensitization is another psychological term that means that there is a "***<u>diminished</u>...<u>emotional re-</u>***<u>*sponsiveness*</u> **to a negative or ADVERSE stimulus** <u>*after...repeated*</u> **exposure to it.**" (Wikipedia.org) This is why there is a surplus of fear-related material in <u>all</u> forms of media. The devil is trying to repeat your exposure level to fear to where, although fear is negative, you will begin to '*accept it*' as a 'normal' part of Life.

The only thing that <u>we</u> are to continually fear is God Himself (Proverbs 9:10). The fear of the LORD is the beginning of wisdom; *knowledge of the Holy One results <u>in</u> understanding.* If your knowledge consists of spells, symbols, chants, charms, 'conferences', ceremonies, chats, 'retreats', rituals, beliefs

& practices that **are** <u>not</u> **related to God's Word**, Will, *or* His Way, your knowledge primarily consists of evil things.

I'm not sure how this sounds to you, but this next statement is revelationally true. **With God, there is no 'gray'**; as the world has lied to you. With God, there is black & white. –Either or. –Two Decisions. God's Way or the devil's way.

<u>Why does the devil</u> *want* **<u>us to become numb to fear?</u>** How can fear-addiction be the devil's gain?

1) <u>Fear is the opposite of faith</u>. We learned in Ingredient/Chapter 4: *Abandonment,* all about faith & how faith is worked by Love. Perfect Love casts **OUT** all fear! (1 John 4:18) If fear is the **<u>opposite</u>** of faith, then operating *in fear* is **contrary** to God's Will. Remember: without faith, it is impossible to please God. (Hebrews 11:6)

2) Fear is a **TRAP**.

Self-created fear without a *confirmed* threat or stimulus (not a movie/TV show depiction/series) holds you internally captive & *prevents* you from taking action.

3) If you get acclimated to fear (scary things) you will *not* be prone to act because your fear-receptor will become dull. **Lack of action** (on your part) gives the devil (the enemy) free course to cause *disorder* in your Life. And you will begin to accept fearful situations as *usual* & *ordinary*.

I pray that I am not going over your head with this, *nor* not making the point effectively understood. Simply put, *the devil* wants us to get *accustomed* to fearful things, **so that we will not be properly conditioned to respond to fear as we** *should*.

God did not give us a spirit of fear; He gave us a spirit of Love, of (His) Power & of a sound (lucid) mind (2 Timothy 1:7). We shouldn't be walking around afraid, **just** to be afraid.

–*Afraid* to tell the Truth. – *Afraid* to get out. –
Afraid to try (for the 1ˢᵗ time or try **again**). – *Afraid* to
start the business. – *Afraid* to confront & address. –
Afraid to apply for the job or the loan. – *Afraid* to
seek reconciliation & **forgiveness**. – *Afraid* to *genuinely* say "I **apologize**. I was sincerely wrong. Please
forgive me."

– *Afraid* to forgive, let go & start over. – *Afraid* to
go to school. – *Afraid* to cut off '*that*' relationship.
– *Afraid* to say no. – *Afraid* to say yes. – *Afraid* to
self-change. – *Afraid* to believe in yourself. – *Afraid*
to believe in others. – *Afraid* to trust in God......all of
these fears (mentioned & unmentioned) are based **on**
thoughts which are connected to **other** thoughts
that are forming a *forged* reality that is *preventing*
some necessary action on *your* part.

Commit to memory point #3: *If you get acclimated
to fear* (scary things) *you won't be prone to act because your fear-receptor will become dull. Lack of
action* (on your part) *gives the devil* (the enemy) *free
course to cause disorder in your Life. And you will*

begin to <u>accept</u> fearful situations as usual & ordinary; when they are **not**.

The **TRAP** of fear is **not** like the needle-incased **TRAP** of *Abandonment,* which was intended for the heart. <u>The **TRAP** of fear is intended for the *brain*</u>. The daunting fact of the matter is that the **TRAP** of fear, *that's intended for the brain,* is **invisible!** The **TRAP** <u>is in the mind,</u> *itself.* (Imagine wide-eyed emoji here)

The only way that we will be able to push past fear with God-like victory is if we confront the fearful thing(s) head on.

***You want to see the movie, but you don't have any one to go with you...GO...TO...THE...MOVIE. Stomp fear in the face & go by *yourself.* Go to a matinee viewing, purchase your ticket, and enjoy the show. (make sure the movie is not an enemy to your spiritual progress & development!) ☺

***That person quit speaking to you & you have **no** idea why?

–pray (before hand) for wisdom & instruction; once you receive from God your answers, go & approach the individual to discover the Truth of the matter.

***Your boss refuses year after year to give you adequate raises? Research & <u>document</u> *evidence* of why you *should be* compensated according to statistical data (your work performance). Pray to God for wisdom in *speech* & conduct (always), set up a meeting time with your boss & *humbly* present your points of interest & information.

***On a more serious note, you have that loved one, who is a drug addict or alcoholic that you've been enabling with money &/or residency? Lift up a <u>new</u> standard. Decree & declare what **will** be in order for you to be an active participant in *their* life. <u>If they chose the addiction over you</u>, courageously take the steps to *remove yourself* from the position of 'enabler'. Refuse to be manipulated & stagnated by fear **anymore**.

Whatever that 'thing' is, that you know NEEDS to be done, but you are somewhat fearful & apprehensive about doing so, gird yourself up in spiritual courageousness (Joshua 1:8)!!! If God is FOR us, then WHO can be against us (successfully)???!!! NOOOOOO ONEEEEEE (Romans 8:31)!

Living in fearful thoughts & *constant,* fearful expectation is <u>not</u> **normal!** Change your mindset from
a victim to a victor. **Take control** over your Life &
the processes within! The first process that you
must take control over is your *thought* processes.
Judge your <u>*every*</u> thought! Take on the mind of
Christ Jesus (CHOOSE to think <u>**as**</u> the Word of God
says we *should;* Romans 12:2; Philippians 2:5). Cast
down (throw out of your mind <u>every</u> time) <u>any</u> & *every*
vain (pointless, contrary) imagination that 'comes' to
you, in the attempt to exalt *that* thought higher
above the thoughts that God's Word says we <u>**are**</u> to
have (2 Corinthians 10:5).

Even though the **TRAP** of fear is invisible & located
within the brain, the **TRAP** is large. It is large because thoughts in your brain shape your Life. As
you think things are is how they are *to you* (Proverbs 23:7). Your thoughts don't make things fact, <u>if</u>
<u>your thoughts are not based on</u> Yahweh God's
Truth.

–But, your belief in *your* thoughts makes your
thoughts <u>***your...***</u> reality. You can think the sky is
green when it's really blue. *Your* belief in what *is*

not true **does not** make your belief valid! Realize that unnecessary fear that <u>is not based on legitimate rationale</u> is a **TRAP** for the mind intended to keep you from *necessary* action.

Analyze your Life. Recognize where you've been walking in circles *because* of the fear to make a *certain* decision. *Your decision to act in spite of* the image of fear is what will break you <u>out</u> of the invisible **TRAP** of fear. And every time you chose to act, *in spite of* fear (which actually equals the definition of courageous) it will be easier to get out of fear's **TRAP** & to STAY out.

What decision will be your **first** attempt at violently getting out of fear's TRAP, while slicing the spirit of *fear's* throat in the process?? (Matthew 11:12)

INGREDIENT SIX

Fantasy-Thinking

My LORD!!! God help us ALL with *this* one, **Jesus!** —Fantasy-thinking.

I am not sure about you, but I've exhausted hours (off & on) of my Life spending time fantasizing. — ESPECIALLY when I am in an undesired circumstance, situation or event. ***Let*** me be **required** to be in some sort of *mandatory*, **extra LONGGG**, *boring* meeting, or any place where my absolute, full attention is not constantly maintained...*GONE*! I'm talking about to and <u>IN</u> another place!!! My imagination is incredibly vivid & my attention span has opportunity for improvement. There have been times where I actually got annoyed when someone interrupted me from my imaginary interactions.

I thought at one point in time that fantasy-thinking was an innocent past-time, a way to pass time along. That fantasy-thinking can be deemed innocent as long as one's thoughts aren't contrary to God's Word or God's desires for us. After all, the Bible says that whatever is *true*, or *noble*, whatever is *right* or *pure*, whatever is *admirable* or *lovely*, if anything is *excellent* or *praise worthy*, then **these** are the things that we should think about (Philippians 4:8).

I thought that it was *excellent* to imagine myself randomly being somewhere & a man walks up to me & tells me that he **knows** by *the Holy Spirit of God* that I am **his** pre-ordained wife. –That he wants to meet my Pastors & my family, get to know me & make 'this thing' official, ASAP (GOD's Way)! And coincidentally every time...(*yes* –I'd have *different* versions of the same fantasy!)...this king-charming of mine would be a doctor, architect, engineer, etc ready to 'sweep me off my feet'. And the beautiful thing about it all was that he **only** wanted to love me & take care of me & for me to love him & take care of him. *Take care of him?!* (...I heard some woman shriek...) Yes! Take care of him!

My king-charming had been hurt, used, abused & misused in his Life. And all he ever wanted was a good woman that was going to be faithful, wise, honest, dedicated, sincere, warm in spirit, compassionate, loving & considerate with, to & *for* him. And God blessed **me** by king-charming finding **me**. Sometimes king-charming & I would sail away on his fully-paid yacht. –Where we would **now** live because he was wealthy & wise & made solid investments. My king-charming only <u>chose</u> to work for community purposes & philanthropy-efforts. *I really could go on & on & onnnnn...*

"King-Charming" is *just one version* of **personal** fantasy-thinking that I've entertained over the years of my Life. You may be questioning "What's *wrong* with fantasy-thinking?"

You know that we have to go to the definition of *fantasy*, right? **WHAT**?! I thought that you *knew* me by now!!! ☺

FANTASY (n): the faculty (the talent) or activity of imagining things, especially things that are impossible or improbable; a fanciful mental image, typically one on which a person dwells *at length* or *repeatedly* & which reflects their conscious or unconscious wishes; an idea with *no basis* <u>in</u> reality.

You still may be asking, "WHAT...is the problem with fantasy-thinking? **The problem with fantasy-thinking is when we do so <u>to the point</u> that we begin to practice** fantasy-*living*, *alienating* reality.

Here comes the glass-house...

During the last 20 years, *(Whoa! –I can really say that now?!)* I have not had great experiences in personal relationships with men. <u>Sadly</u> & <u>upsettingly</u>, it seemed at one point that the only men that found 'interest' in me were married men. These would be married men that, for *whatever* reason (there are too many reasons to name), were willing to step *out-*

side of the sanctity of their marriage to obtain intimacy from a stranger.

Being around (mostly) men the majority of my life, I generally know what men want, like & think. My time spent with them 99% of my Life *granted* me this 'inside' knowledge. One of my favorite, personal sayings to men (who have been close associates) over these years has been, "...*JUST treat me like one of the guys*..." And I MEANT IT when I said it to men, **every** time.

Various conversations with disgruntled married men were like flies talking to a Venus-fly trap. I'd literally had to have *mercy* on them & send them on their way because I could '*see*' that they wanted to be 'devoured'. My straight-forward nature *eliminated* the usual domestic-guessing games that they *detested* & coincidently *heightened* their attraction level. But, because of wanting to maintain <u>some</u> sort of the morals that those who reared me tried to instill in me, (I didn't want to be a mistress) I played '*stupid*' concerning their advances.

One day, after the '*heart-break that broke the camel's back*', I decided, '*Forget about it*'. IF I DO involve myself with a married man, I do not have to worry about him pretending to be faithful to me. I decided that I didn't want to be a home-wrecker; I didn't want anyone to leave their wife *for me*. I just wanted occasional affection & (unrealized *then*)...**pretend**-love.

There was a man that I came to know, through un-disclosed means. We became close & **not** for any underlying malicious, motive on *either* of our parts. We interacted when necessary. As we all know, the more time that you spend with someone, the more things you end up sharing with them. Through con-versations, this married man revealed that he was married & that they were constantly fighting, year after year. This particular day was a day where he & his wife had a big falling out.

I was **always** the type to try to help the man see **the other** side of the situation that he couldn't/wouldn't see. I **never** bashed the wife (even if what the man said she 'did' '*seemed*' horrible). And if *anything*, I tried to be the voice **for** her (not wanting OR need-ing neither awards nor honor from ANYone!). I tried to give reasons why he *should* go back & try again with his spouse.

During this conversation on *this* particular day, this
man was actually crying. I do not mean a tear or
two, but actually talking with tears falling out of his
eyes for a great length of time. I could not believe it.
He was very vulnerable, *unashamed* & decided to
'let his hair' completely '...down'. <u>I **never** knew a
man to be so emotionally honest *without* prompting,
prodding or provoking</u>.

He shared his hurts, frustrations, fears, desires, apprehensions, anger, etc. It was as if I had a psychia-
trist's couch in front of me & he laid down & let it
all go. I ended up crying with him as *he* cried &
shared his *secret* pain from his years of silence. I
<u>tried</u> to help him find a way to resolve, to make
some attempt to go back home & '*try, try again*'. At
the end of the conversation, he said that he tried all
that he could & that he was going to stay until his
child could understand why he was leaving.

Even then, and **after** that conversation, nothing
'happened' between us. I *knew* that he was attracted
to me & I was attracted to him. But like I said earlier, I was raised & taught that adultery was wrong.
It's CLEARLY & unavoidably stated in the Bible.
But due to <u>certified</u> circumstances, he & I <u>had</u> to be

involved with each other, which required more time to be spent together. After quite some time, he let me know that he was 'interested' in me & that he wanted to be 'intimate'. I actually turned him down for **years**. Then after that '*heart-ache that broke the camel's back*', I rationalized to myself, 'Why not?'

ALBEIT <u>very</u> wrong, we 'did' it. *I was completely convicted.* I could not do it anymore & I told him so. We maintained our friendship & interacted as our responsibilities required. Even though, we didn't do 'it' again, we became closer & closer through time. After a while, he told me that he wished he had known that he was going to meet me before meeting his wife, so that he could have waited for me.

Most people may think that this was just a 'line' that he gave me. And I can understand why they would think so. But I <u>know</u> that he was genuine. It's **very** *rare* how real, honest & open *this* man's heart was. VERY rare; which is *actually* why I was attracted to him.

Through time, as conversations continued on, he told me over & over again that he was leaving his wife once his child got old enough to understand. I _never_ asked him to leave. I _never_ asked him to tell me that he was leaving. He always _volunteered_ this information in his moments of sharing arguments & personal frustrations; as if he was trying to console & convince _himself_ that he was eventually departing. I **continued** <u>to try to give him advice on **staying**</u> & making it work _with_ his wife. Through many years, we became great friends. YET...After a while, I (eventually) began **imagining** what life would be like _as_ his wife.

THE FANTASY-THINKING ENSUED!
I started meditating & envisioning all kinds of situations that involved me & him & a fabulous future. Our disagreements were even lovingly had (the disagreements in my fantasies). The problem with this & the **general problem** with fantasy-thinking _altogether_ is that it **wastes time** on unrealistic, unproductive situations!

FANTASY (n): the faculty (the talent) or activity of imagining things, especially things that are impossible or improbable; a fanciful mental image, typically one on which a person dwells at length or repeatedly & which reflects their conscious or unconscious wishes; <u>an idea with no basis in reality.</u>

While I was wasting time imagining about life with him once his child was old enough to realize what was really going on, Life was passing **me** by. I was spending time thinking & imagining about things that **weren't probable**! It COULDDDD happen. But *really?* Gamble on life like *that?* Wait for door #6 & hope that it opens ***for me*** 5 years from then? No! I've gambled enough.

As we all should know by now, Life is filled with de-tails that require our (spiritual & natural) attention at all times. When we have families, our time is now divided to where we have to divvy our thought-time to each individual & correlating circumstance to make sure that proper attention is being paid; no 'stone left unturned'. If we are **TRAP**PED in fanta-sy-thinking, **what** & *who* is being neglected by us?

There is NO commodity more valued than the earthly concept of **time**.

Reiterating the importance of realizing responsibil-ity, the devil (the enemy of man) would want nothing MORE than for you (us) to waste minutes, hours, days, months, years, EVEN decades of your Life...fantasizing about things that *probably are <u>not</u>* going to occur.

Us being made in God's image & likeness means that we have the **creative power** to cause things to exist. When we turn our thoughts into actions, – actions that take form from our personal vision & plan(s), we can do **anything** with **God's endorsement!** When we think on things *idly*, with no intended purpose or plan, we are now allowing & inviting our minds to become the playground for the devil. Have you heard of the saying "...an idle mind is the devil's workshop"? Well, this is ever true.

Lost focus –misdirected thoughts & *unplanned* **living is what the devil wants from you/us.** If you are off focus, you won't be tapped into the spiritual realm, being connected to God through & by His Holy Spirit & <u>you will not know</u> what it is that you *should* pray for (Romans 8:26) –which MORE THAN LIKELY will be something AGAINST the kingdom of darkness.

I have been so consumed with my personal thoughts & situations at various moments in my life. It was during these moments the devil saw opportunity & simultaneously, the devil snuck into the cracks of the lives of my loved ones, trying to sow seeds of hell & torment in their spirits & lives. I was too self-consumed & was not on my spiritual watch (Habakkuk 2:1). I allowed havoc to spiritually-sneak past me & to even enter *my own* Life. As God's kings & priests in the earth (Revelation 1:6; Revelation 5:10), we are called to be intercessors for God's people & God's Plan in the earth. **If you are stuck in 'La-La land' fantasizing about 'who knows what', <u>what things are spiritually running rampant around you</u>?**

How many options is the world currently providing for you to 'lose' yourself & 'escape' reality via fantasy-avenues? There are now virtual games where you can 'create' 'lives' from virtual scratch. –Even down to planned penny-pinching, progressive play-dates, purchasing pets & planting produce. BUT TIME MUST BE INVESTED in order to keep these virtual-gigs going. OR if that gig isn't interesting enough, you can attempt to be your *own* celebrity – seeking to be followed by any & everyone through social media. You can make your number of 'Likes'

& number of 'Friends' your **new** motive & drive for promotional actions & displayed content. You can now live your life spending minutes birthed into hours coddling cyberspace concerning your crafted concoctions in hopes that you create a hunger in others that makes *your* social-status climb. OR you can lose yourself in hard-core games where murdering people can be done on colossal, high-definition flat-screens, while being bathed in surround-sound. You can even compete with others across the globe to see who the best 'legal', virtual-murderer is. Games are 'innocent', after all...

Let's not forget the crude & vulgar side of fantasy-thinking.

The devil **loves** this side: where 'A' through 'D' –list celebrities are super-paid for Godless-exhibitionism, porn-stars reign on high & teens in 'teen-like' shows (*you know* the Networks responsible) & 'teen-like' programs are trying to make a *covert*, futuristic, sexual name for themselves.

Fantasy-thinking, depending on desire, (vain imaginations; 2 Corinthians 10:5; James 1:5) can lead someone to insane, illicit paths of meditating on bestiality, incest or pedophilia. Or fantasy-thinking can cause you to devalue the sanctity of marriage where you & your spouse begin to seek 'swinging' with strangers. <u>Even if no direct action</u> is taken according to *your* fantasy-like thoughts, your <u>creative mind</u> (intended to be creative for God's Purposes & Will in the earth) <u>is being misused & mishandled</u>, *all to* the devil's extreme enjoyment. And...it can only occur through *our* mental participation...

The major point that will override & overrule any other topic of interest at <u>any</u> given time is that we are <u>in</u> a SPIRITUAL <u>**WAR**</u> *for* SOULS (this includes our *own* soul). This is true regardless of WHAT you believe. –Regardless of religious belief or the lack *of* it. Since the devil himself knows in (whatever has replaced) his heart, that he is not able to contend with Yahweh God our Creator, the only way that the devil ***can try*** to get to back at God is by influencing God's people to turn *away* from Him. Just like my Apostle Jacqueline Clark says, "...the devil uses the same trick ever since the Garden of Eden..."

Wouldn't YOU consider that an insult: if you were absolutely Holy & ALL Powerful & you put yourself in a Body Form so that you could offer Yourself to be the Holy Sacrifice to be offered up to your 'Omnipresent' Self for the Atonement for the sins of ALL of man-kind...*only* for the <u>ones</u> that you died & resurrected <u>Yourself</u> for... to go about *whoring* after other gods?! (Judges 2:17)

***Influencing you to act OUTSIDE of the image & likeness of God **will always** be the tactic the devil uses ON you/us **to try to use <u>you/us,</u>** to get *back* at God. ***

Quit tying the devil's puppets strings on **your** brain, shoulders & arms. We <u>**can**</u> have control over our **<u>own</u>** minds. <u>YES</u>!!! It is going to take EXTREME work, due diligent work. Every thought you/we have will <u>have</u> to be judged *personally* according to the Word of God. God-less thoughts, *we* <u>will</u> have to renounce! **<u>Fantasy-thinking is not innocent if God's Purpose is not attached to it</u>**!!! This is what God showed me...We have to stop tricking *ourselves.*

Fantasy-thinking <u>is not</u> mere imagining. **<u>Fantasy-thinking is being LOST in thoughts that are ultimately unproductive for God's Kingdom Purposes</u>**.

Whatever is true, or noble, whatever is right or pure, whatever is admirable or lovely, if anything is excellent or praise worthy, *then these* are the things that we *should* think about (Philippians 4:8).

The things that we think about should be relational to somehow advancing ourselves, our loved ones & ALL of God's Kingdom citizens, TOWARD the Glory of God. Not *understanding* this, not complying *with* this or *choosing to not believe* this, will keep you bound in a *mirage*-like **TRAP**.

Fantasy-like thoughts **can be** considered addictive, especially when you do not like your current situation(s) & look to fantasy-thinking as an *escape*. But I promise you, freedom in your spirit is even MORE attractive! Freedom in your spirit comes when you **choose to live your Life based on God's Truth!!!**

Chose to <u>loose</u> yourself from idle, *selfish* thinking. Decide to be enthusiastically devoted to *purposed, proper* thoughts. Being adamant about doing so, will keep you freed from this fantasy-**TRAP** forever!

Reality AND Life are waiting for you (us) to 'grab the reigns' of (y)our mind & TAKE CHARGE, according to God's Word. God's Power to do so is accessible to you. **The individual that can control his (own) <u>body</u>**...is STRONGER than ANY person who is strong enough to overtake a *city* (Proverbs 16:32).

Learn from me.
Let's not waste **any** more time. Let us lay aside *every* weight & *every* high thought that tried (& tries...) to exalt itself *in our minds* against the Knowledge of Christ Jesus. **ESCAPE** fantasy-futile-thinking *today* (1 Corinthians 10:13)...

Look! –the **TRAP** is *now* open............

INGREDIENT SEVEN

Settle-Mind-Set

(Low Self-Worth!...How were YOU reared/programmed?)

Philippians 1:9-11 (ESV) says, "And it is my prayer that your love may abound more & more, with knowledge & all discernment, (10) so that you may approve what is excellent, & so be pure & blameless for the day of Christ, (11) filled with the fruit of righteousness that comes through Jesus Christ, to the glory & praise of God."

My pastors mentioned this scripture to our congregation in reference to verse 10 sometime during this year (while writing this: *currently* Nov. 2014).

Apostle Kelso Clark & Apostle Jacqueline Clark said that "we cannot approve something to be excellent until we **become** excellent ourselves". And this makes absolute sense. *How can you recognize & identify something that you have no knowledge of?*

When you have a mindset that is willing to settle for *un*satisfactory people, *un*satisfactory places & *un*satisfactory processes, you do not have an excellent spirit. (Help us, oh God...) Those with *excellent spirits* **cannot** accept things that are *less* than adequate, <u>if</u> their personal choice is involved & *allowed* to reign in the situation.

SETTLE (v.): (meaning for **this** context) to accept or agree to (something that one considers to be *less* than satisfactory).

People who have a settle-mind-set <u>CANNOT</u> have excellent spirits. To have an excellent spirit means <u>also</u> that you have knowledge, understanding &/or wisdom to solve problems or know how to seek those who *do* solve situations (Daniel 5:12). Having a **settle**-(*acceptant of the <u>unsatisfactory</u>*)-**mind**-set is *a problem itself.*

God pointed something out to me when I just went back to review what He had me write. It's in relation to the scripture in Philippians that we opened this ingredient/chapter-exposure with.

> Philippians 1:9-11 (ESV) says, "And it is my prayer that your love may abound more & more, with knowledge & all discernment, (10) so that you may approve what is excellent, & so be pure & blameless for the day of Christ, (11) filled with the fruit of righteousness that comes through Jesus Christ, to the glory & praise of God."

The particular verse that God highlighted in my mind is verse 9 in direct relation to verse 10. Verse 9 summarizes that the author Paul prayed that the love of the people (us) would thrive (prosper in spite of challenges) more & more. This prospering love that Paul was praying for us to have, he was **also** praying that our <u>love would be **connected** to knowledge & all discernment</u> *(**Discernment** is the ability to <u>judge well</u>; or perception in the absence of* *judgment, with a view to obtaining spiritual direction & understanding).* Now here is the *'kic-kah' (kicker)*: Verse 10 of Philippians 1 suggests strongly that **knowing** what is excellent...COMES FROM having a love that prospers & *that* love being **connected** to knowledge & discernment!

This is an absolute Rhema-Word downloading right now. (Rhema Word is a verse, portion of Scripture or an imparted Word that the Holy Spirit brings to our attention with application to a current situation or need for direction.) This is not the direction that I thought God was going to take me (us) when originally beginning explaining this ingredient/chapter. But this revelation is SO PROFOUND. WE have to go deeper.

The equational map in Philippians 1 verse 9 & 10 looks like this:
Love that abounds + Abounding Love that's <u>connected</u> to knowledge & discernment = an EXCELLENT SPIRIT

'What ?!
Are you sitting shocked as well? If not, then congratulations. You are more in tune with the heart & desires of our Father God, which does not negative-

ly reflect upon the rest of us. The remainder of us will not be discouraged as we go further with the Holy Spirit, so that we can detect & get closer to the heart beat of God. This is God's Will for us, *after all...*

Paul said he was praying for our love to abound, **WITH** knowledge & discernment, SO THAT we may APPROVE what is EXCELLENT. The statement is cause & effect. –Relative to the college course *LOGIC.* <u>**IF**</u> we possess love that abounds; *abounding love that is connected to knowledge & discernment,* <u>**THEN**</u> we will be able to approve (recognize & endorse) what is **excellent**. It may sound as if I am repeating myself, but we must 'get' this into our spirits.

The first thought that came to me once God dropped this revelation into my spirit, was that if we do not possess love that is abounding (love that is *flourishing*), then more than likely we are stuck in the **TRAP** indicated in Ingredient/Chapter 3: *The Difference between Self Concept & Self-Esteem.* The devil would like for life to condition us to think that because bad things happen 'to' us & people walked out 'on' us or people deceived, used &/or *abandoned* us (Ingredient/Chapter4), then we somehow are not loved. And *this* thought leads to the thought that because these love-less situations manifested, then we need to not (fully) love others, in an *attempt to protect* ourselves.

The *inadequacy* **of others to properly love you <u>does not</u> mean that you have to shut off <u>your</u> faith-initiator.** Faith is WORKED *by* love (Galatians 5:6). And remember without **<u>REAL</u>** faith (=faith that is worked *by* love), it is *impossible* to please God (Hebrews 11:6). Do you <u>see</u> the **TRAP?**

The TRAP= Get hurt » stop loving » stop believing in Love » (inadvertently) stop pleasing God...

YOU <u>ARE</u> LOVE because God is *in* you (1 John 4:8) & GOD <u>IS</u> LOVE (God is in you to dwell if you've fully accepted Christ Jesus as your **Lord** & your Savior-Romans 10:9).

You are WORTHY of Love in spite of the *deficiencies of Love* **that other people own**. You have to be built up in your self-concept & self-esteem! **Your** worth is not a reflection of what *that* person or *those* people did to you. <u>What they did to you is a direct reflection of the Truth that *they are detached* from; the true image & likeness of God.</u> **What they did to you...ended the mirage-like farce that they were trying to** *convince* <u>**you**</u> **of &** **manipulate** <u>**you**</u> *with.*

That person or those people who were selfishly & coldly inconsiderate to you only showed you that ***THEY*** <u></u> have the LOVE issue. You can walk away with dignity knowing that you ARE & should still BE & operate IN Love (operate in God). When you REALIZE & UNDERSTAND that YOU are LOVE *yourself* & that you should not shut off LOVE within you because of the mistreatment from others, **then** you will be properly positioned to seek God for the NEXT level...*Love that abounds.*

Side bar Note:
I am really thanking God right now that He is breaking this 'Love'-thing down for me (us). Seeking Love & receiving mistreatment from people has been an ongoing battle for some time now in my Life. I've yo-yoed between loving & shutting myself

*off from people for decades. Attempts at loving seemed so trivial when it came to thinking about survival & protection of one's self. But I now know that true, pure (not lewd) pleasure & joy can only come from pleasing God our Father, **first** (Matthew 6:33). I understand now that He is giving me (us) the road map to break FREE from the devil's love-lies, spiritual schemes & tantalizing **TRAPs**. We are WELL on our way!!! HALLELUJAH!*

Once we get over the pain & gain fresh Godly perspective on the Purpose & ideology of Love (which is God *Himself*), then we can take on the assignment of possessing Love that abounds (grows). The thing that I think is SO BEAUTIFUL in verse 9 of Philippians 1 is that Paul prayed that our abounding love *should be* **connected** with knowledge & discernment.

THIS... dear one...has been our issue. **We have Loved** *without* **attaching our Love to knowledge & discernment.** We have invested our Love **without** seeking God on the **appropriate** targets & boundaries. We have Loved *aimlessly*, due to low self-esteem & low self-concept. We have settled for pretend-love & counterfeit compassion just so that we can have moments where our *bodies* & *psyches* are not alone; although the company that we have kept has been spiritually-miles away from positively connecting to either or.

We have not understood that we ourselves <u>are</u> Love & that we **do not need** someone to give us that which we *already* are. Notice, the word 'need' was used. Yes! It is nice to have someone to share & reciprocate TRUE Love with. But because we ARE Love, because God is *in* us, because we *are* in God, we are neither depleted nor inadequate because of not having a human to 'give' us Love. God, being thoughtful & kind, Loves us *through* people, anyway. If anyone **truly** Loves you, it is *through* God's Love that they are doing so.

The Holy Spirit, our TRUE, Best Friend –if we will *allow* Him to be, WILL lead us into ALL Truth!!! John 16:13 can be SO REAL for you! God has made it absolutely real for me! As I mentioned to you prior, I prayed & asked God to show me ALWAYS the true hearts of all humans, young & old; **even** if they are fake-smiling in my face & giving me pat-OR-

squeeze-the-back-hugs. –Regardless of gender, title
or circumstance. I asked God to never let me be deceived & to always show me whose heart is genuinely for me & whose heart is **secretly** *against* me,
allowing me to be 100% sure of what God reveals to
me. **AND GOD HAS DONE SO & CONTINUES TO
DO SO**, without fail!!! God is ever faithful concerning this!!!

Seeking God for answers, guidance & direction will
give you the *knowledge* & *discernment* that is needed to connect with the Love that God <u>wants</u> to grow
within you. **Knowledge & discernment** (from God)
**will be the protection necessary to make your Love
flourish** (abound).

With most plants, some sort of pruning is necessary.
According to an online publication "**The Columbi-
an**" (<u>www.columbian.com/</u> article written by Robb
Rosser; 4-25-13), "*the general purpose of pruning
is not to reduce the size of a plant that has grown
too large. Pruning stimulates growth. Weak growth
can be stimulated to grow vigorously by hard cut-
ting back & light pruning best checks vigorous
growth. Pruning...helps establish the shape of a
plant along its natural lines, helps improve flower or*

fruit production [&/or] helps control the time of bloom..."

When what we *thought* was Love gets 'cut' or 'removed' from our Lives without our desire for it to occur, **shift** your perception to believe that it is the work of our Master Creator *pruning us*. Trust that Jehovah God, who made us for **His** Perfect Will & Purpose, KNOWS what our 'natural lines' are. God <u>knows</u> how our lives *should* be shaped. God knows the rate that **He** wants us to grow. Yahweh is well aware of how much needs to be cut back off our Lives so that we can grow at full force, *unhindered*. Because God's Love <u>is</u> Love that abounds & God's Love is <u>connected</u> to knowledge & discernment, **God is more than able to approve what is excellent for US & our Lives.** Do you spiritually 'see' this? Can we agree on this?!

Noooooooooooo; It will not always feel good when what we *thought* was a *part* of us gets removed & we see it lying on the ground OR someone *else* walking off with 'it'. But the only way that we are going to be able to move forward with peace in our hearts is to *fully* decide to TRUST that God knows

what is best for us. <u>Stop settling for that less-than-
satisfactory-'*branch*' because you are **familiar** with it!</u>
When we allow God to prune us, THEN our Love
will flourish & our Love will look like what He
knows our Love *should* look like. Our Love should
look like **Him**! –We are His image & likeness, *remember*? (Genesis 1:27)

Once we allow God to cut away the people, places &
processes that have & **will** hinder our Love-growth,
we are **now** in the position for our Love to abound at
full speed!!! And it is at THIS point, that we must
seek God for His knowledge & His discernment.

<u>KNOW...that the devil</u> (the enemy of man) <u>is **not**
going to sit back idly watching you become more
like God</u>. (...insert big-eyed emoji)

The devil does not want you/us to reach, nor become the fullness of Who God is in the earth (Ephesians 3:19)! The fullness of God comes from
experiencing and *BEING* the Love of Christ *in the
earth*! The devil will do what he has *always* done;
which is try at all times that he is permitted (by
God) to discourage you, influence you to doubt

God's Word & tempt you to cast your pearls before swine (Matthew 7:6); all of which is permitted so that you can be **proven** to be God's *genuine* best (just like Job, in the Bible). The enemy wants to take the new-beauty that God has transformed from your past-ashes (Isaiah 61:3) & get you to *squander* your *newness* on deceptive, manipulative, *puppeteering* demons.

OH YES!

The wolf is *not* easily detected, as I once thought. Do not think that just because 'they' can prophesy that this means that 'they' do not have a two-timing, triple-life-style-having, secretive, spiritual nature that they operate in... (someone needed to hear that). It doesn't matter how long you've *known* them, how much they make you laugh, how much they've been *there* for you, or how much they *understand* you. The devil studies us **TO**...understand us.

I thought since I was somewhat street-wise, the devil couldn't swindle me with his spiritual tricks. HA! The devil **knows** how to look like & sound *just* like a 'saint'. The devil *knows* how to **falsely** project images that he knows YOU like, THROUGH peo-

ple. The devil **knows** the Word of God, after all. The
ONLY WAY that you are going to be able to *detect*
demonic spirits in *this* hour is if you are diligently
cultivating <u>*your*</u> <u>relationship</u> **with God**, *Who will in
turn* whisper to your spirit the devil's plots & ploys
in...particular...people, *especially* those <u>closest</u> to
you.

With God's knowledge & discernment, <u>you will be</u>
<u>**more** than able</u> (Ephesians 3:20) to decipher what's
hidden behind dialogue & deeds. God will give you
clues in your spirit about undisclosed, *unseen*
things. God will speak to you in your slumber with
dreams & visions & give **you** the interpretation upon awakening (if you ask Him to & believe that God
is able to do so). God will warn you of those (people
& situations) that are **not** to be trusted. God will tell
you what decisions you *should* make if you ask Him
for Divine Direction. (Proverbs 3: 4-6) <u>Our</u> **respon-**
sibility in ALL of this is to make sure that *we* trust
what God is telling us & act *according* to the
knowledge that He reveals to us through His Holy
Spirit.

God kept showing me **for four years** that someone
that I trusted was a liar & a master manipulative-

deceiver. For FOUR YEARS God kept speaking to me in my dreams & offering me red flags (while I was awake) to lead me off of & away from the path that was connected to this person. But I rationalized & excused myself <u>out</u> of **believing** that what God was revealing *(spiritually & naturally)* to me was true!

I chose to believe what the person *said*...instead of what the person was actually **showing** me! I had the knowledge of Truth, but I didn't have the correlating, **required**, spiritual discernment. Spiritual discernment would have enabled me to recognize whether or not what the individual was saying & living was true. Knowledge *coupled* with God-given discernment would have allowed me to **properly** be able to determine whether or not this person operated in integrity that was excellent.

What was the *first* problem?
I **settled** for what was less than satisfactory. I *agreed* to accept treatment that was *not* up to par. I **decided** to stay connected to <u>someone who did not operate in God's image & likeness</u> ('behind closed doors'). This alone, was a strong indication of a trick of the devil.

1 Corinthians 13 tells us explicitly what Love is about. When a relationship, platonic or more, does not have the two participants **reciprocate** the Love that this chapter of scripture instructs Love *should* be, your awareness is open & you have to make a God-like Decision to *separate. —Even if it's your best friend of the last 26 years...*

<u>Knowledge</u> & <u>discernment</u> is going to come from knowing what God's Word says & applying God's Word to your Life. When you know God's Word, you know God's Will. God's Word is going to be the Measuring Stick for what is acceptable in our Lives. God's Truth (His Word) is the **only way** that we are going to be able to determine what IS *actually* excellent & worthy of our (God's) approval.

The equational map in Philippians verse 9 & 10 looks like this:
Love that abounds + Abounding Love that's connected to knowledge & discernment = an EXCELLENT SPIRIT

We have to stop **creating** & *accepting* excuses for people, places & processes that are divisive **TRAP**s *purposed...*to stunt our **Love**-growth by *some* means. Although we may find ourselves in a position where we are wronged or unconsidered by another individual or a set of people, you are going to HAVE to submit your heart to God & seek God on HOW to <u>not</u> allow your heart to become cold. You are also going to have to seek The Holy Spirit on how to not allow *your* decisions (& mindset) to put you in a similar circumstance again.

Time & time again,
...we are going to have to find a way to forgive, move forward & Love *yet* again. But THANKFULLY, <u>Loving does not require us to be fools!!!!!</u> Discretion is desired. Wise counsel is imperative. We must unite the Love that we ARE (the Love that God gave us <u>to</u> be) with knowledge AND discernment. **Knowledge & discernment from God will be the holy safeguards that will shield our hearts & prune our lives from deceitful wickedness.**

Deciding to **BE** Love (<u>not</u> *look* for Love), **agreeing** with God's Plan to make *His* Love <u>in</u> you flourish & attaching knowledge & discernment with your growing Love...generates the excellent spirit that will be required if you (we) intend to stay out of the settle-mind-set **TRAP**. It is only he/she that has an *excellent spirit* that will have the *discernment* to 'see' &/or 'sense' the **TRAP** & avoid it all-together.

Let's 'ditch' what is *familiar* & walk with a **new** desire for <u>**excellent**</u> things, <u>**excellent**</u> people, <u>**excellent**</u> processes, and <u>**excellent**</u> spirits. Let us extract ALL excuses! Remember: we...especially our decisions...<u>must be excellent *first*</u>.

Are you willing to do the <u>work</u> necessary to stay OUT of *this* **TRAP**?

INGREDIENT EIGHT

Single-Parent Homes &

Double-Parent Homes

That Lack Parental Unity

Before we begin this ingredient/chapter, please know that there is no need to tense or tighten up. **The points discussed here <u>will not</u> be from a judgmental standpoint.** The points will be discussed from an *awareness* point of view. I have *personal, proximal* <u>experience</u> with both the single-parent home & the double parent home that lacks parental unity. Therefore, I know certain, intimate repercussions of both environments.

As with this entire book, I am sharing portions of *my* Life (even if not directly stated) & walking WITH you through this process of realization, deliverance & freedom from the devil's slippery **TRAPs.**

A defensive standpoint **must not** be enacted by you, in your spirit. *Denial,* laced with the self-deceiving spirit of *pride,* will *always* be a few of the largest strongholds to encounter in *any* given situation in our lives (*Denial* & *Pride* are fueled by the **TRAPs** of *Fear* & *Doubt,* which we've already covered). Embracing *awareness* is the *antidote* that remedies self-deception.

Look at this ingredient/chapter's concepts from an objective standpoint. Afterwards, seek The Holy Spirit on your *personal* path to resolution & fortitude. God alone, knows the way(s) that we should take (Job 23:10). Our process & progressive paths are all different. Yet, in our different circumstances, God's Wisdom is *unchanging.* He is **Omniscient** (All-Knowing), **Omnipresent** (everywhere at all times) & **Omnipotent** (All-Powerful). God, the Great I AM, is Supreme enough to help us all on an *individual* basis, *collectively.*

However, we must *permit* God to reign in our situation by **surrendering our will** to His Word (His Way). Let's dive into the first subject matter of single-parent homes.

SINGLE-PARENT HOMES:

There are various & NUMEROUS reasons why single-parent homes are instigated. **Outside of a death**, decisions that result in single-parent homes are weighty ones. **When it comes to the result of the severance**, more than likely one parent (or both) is the subject matter for self-concern. *The substantial, futuristic, spiritual **focus**, <u>however</u>, lies upon the child(ren), even if this is not realized.*

A single-parent home, from the devil's standpoint, is a *tasty* **TRAP**.

–God intended for child-rearing to be a **shared** experience; with two parents participating in the cultivation of *their* produced seed. Single-parents have the **hardest** job because there is no one to walk beside you & support the **weight** of the <u>assignment</u> of raising your child(ren) to walk in God's image & likeness in the earth...if you are *even* <u>knowledgeable</u>

enough to KNOW that this NEEDS to be accomplished.

Single-parents must work full time in order to offer provision (if they are <u>not</u>: choosing to live off of the government's poverty-producing system, nor receiving wealthy income from a financial-sponsor). Generally, the single-parent has to be the sole caretaker, while looking for catered ways (if they are inspired to do so) to upgrade oneself so that their household can stand, in spite of ever-increasing financial demands. The single-parent has to be the solitary intercessor; decreeing & declaring wisdom & protection over your child(ren)'s life (lives), again...if they are spiritually AWARE enough to even do so. But the devil is **counting** (& hoping) on the single-parent being so <u>overwhelmed with</u> <u>*providing*</u>, that they **spiritually** & **naturally neglect** their seed---ushering the child(ren) into the (spiritual & natural) devices of our wicked enemy, satan (lower-case '*s*'intentional).

NOTE: Single-parents must know…just because you financially provide for your child(ren) does <u>not</u> mean that you are 'doing' more than enough for your offspring. This is good info for those parents that do not have full custody, but are paying child support. Although financial support for children is to be expected, reality reveals that financial support isn't generally guaranteed. Just because you are being financially responsible for your offspring, does not mean that you deserve awards or accolades. Children are your responsibility & most responsibilities (these days) require finances. *However,* money feeds neither the psyche, nor the soul.

<u>It is DANGEROUS to raise your child(ren) & not be concerned about **how, when, where & why** they think *what* they think</u> (even at a young age). –To raise **complete** *strangers* in your home with secret thoughts & feelings, living under *your* roof –just a bedroom away… –To have **no idea** who their influences are or what are their peer-pressured preferences. It is understood that a single-parent, as the sole-household-*human*-provider, must get adequate

rest so that those long, strenuous hours of working can be tackled night after night or day after day. But your child(ren) spending the majority of *their* time with *you* being 'quiet' so you can lecture &/or 'rest', isn't wise. Without *your* parental, *Godly*-influence, your child(ren) will become the devil's playground.

The world *itself* will be a demonic circus filled with dressed-up clowns (wolves in sheep clothing), evil charades (sugar-coated mind-control), poisoned candy (sex, drugs & alcohol) & slave-like, sinful hobbies awaiting their curiosity & acceptance.

The devil, the enemy of man, will **always** go after the offspring, the NEXT generation! Every sector of human kind has a generational curse that the devil has intended to be individually transferred to & through *every* individual of the next generation. The devil will **always** try to take the focus off of the necessary, *nurturing* aspect that is *required* in the spiritual warfare for your child(ren)'s soul(s)!

Parental nurturing (activated through *quality* time spent WITH the child) is a preventative, protective measure that is often over-looked, even if inadvert-ently done. Knowing your child's favorite color, favorite TV show, favorite outfit or favorite meal is not parental nurturing.

Science & psychology have the on-going debate of '*nurture vs. nature*'. If this topic is being introduced for the first time, *this debate is in reference to which influence is predominant in the outcome of a child's personality & behavioral makeup.* '*Nurture*' refers to the time that is spent on *application* to the child's perception of Life &/or the *lack* of application. '*Nature*' refers to what environment(s) the child has encountered &/or been exposed to. These environments are thought to represent influences that potentially <u>condition</u> the child in *thoughts, decisions* & *deeds*. The on-going question in this debate is: 'Which **influence** is most pivotal?'

The God-like answer: '**nurture**' & '**nature**' **are both critical.** Time spent in shaping & filtering the child's mind & spirit is important, where as the proper environment is significant as well. <u>What good is there to</u>: 1) have a parent that is lovingly spending time with the child, trying to make sure the devil hasn't planted any negative seeds into their mind or their soul, while the child is in an environment where there's a high probability for physical, verbal, emotional, psychological, &/or spiritual abuse? Or: 2) there's no abuse that the child may encounter, but concurrently there is no physical, verbal, emotional, psychological, &/or spiritual *nurturing* taking place? The child is **fed**, **warm**, **clean** & **safe**, but is thoroughly neglected & left to entertain one's self within the confines of the home, while the parent has 'work' to do. It may not look like it...but this is a **TRAP** (for the child).

These two situations listed prior, although on opposite sides of the spectrum, they are both concerns for a negative, spiritual-*setup*. Overlooking the child's need for personality & spiritual cultivation & focusing *only* on the child obeying your chores & requests (if you even place ANY upon them), sets THEM up for the **TRAP**s we've already covered in Ingredients/Chapters 1-7. Think about it...It all stems from what WE were introduced to (or NOT introduced) **as children!!!** –That's where the **TRAP**s were ALL **laid**---in ALL of our childhoods!

It is best to start cultivating your relationship with your child(ren) when they are **young**. *How*? Truly being concerned with their opinions & tracking their thought patterns. As a parent, you make strides to have *conversations* with your child so that you can *discover* HOW they are *prone* to make decisions. As a caretaker, be humble enough to admit when you are *wrong* & _apologize_ for not getting it all right. **This will teach your child to do the very same.**

Ultimately, make a definitive stand to NOT CARRY ON A GENERATIONAL CURSE OF '*just do as I say*'-ness. This type of child-rearing is not loving. Love is the thing that will outlast any situation & will endure all things (1 Corinthians 13:7).

Your child(ren) may be a teenager now & you feel like all hope is lost. I will tell you first hand that all hope is NOT lost. My mother & I had an absolute, horrible time in our relationship while I was a teenager. I ended up going through a harder time when I left home after graduating high school. My mother & I didn't speak for **years**; I was not sure if she really knew if I was alive, then. But the one thing I KNOW made a difference in my Life was that she (& others) prayed for me.

The effective, fervent prayer of the righteous avails much (James 5:16). <u>It is all about</u> 1) your *personal* relationship with Yahweh, Our Father God *(is your spiritual relationship with God superficially-'surface' only?)*, 2) you seeking to maintain holy, clean **hands** (& Life & heart), & 3) your confidence level of God inside of *yourself.*

There are so many scriptures in the Bible that pertain to the seed of the righteous being protected & blessed. In these moments of contradiction where it 'seems' like the devil is winning, this is the opportune moment for you to exercise your God-given authority as king & priest in the earth & pray & declare what WILL be for the Life (Lives) of your child(ren). **Then** seek God on what positive, nurturing seeds **you** can sow in the life of your child(ren) so that one day reconciliation & resolution can flow out of *their* hearts.

*****<u>*Here's a secret*</u>: most children are not honest with their parents &/or do not come to their parents for resolution because they feel that their parents **will not be aware** or **<u>HONEST</u>** about <u>their *own* personal, *parental* role</u> (responsibility/contribution) for what *has* occurred. This is <u>not</u> a session to blame parents; this is an opportunity to close up breaches. A child's heart will be softened *quicker* when the parent(s) can be willing to **murder** the spirit of pride within *themselves*.

Twenty years later, after much anguish & prickly tears, I can say that *finally* my mother & I are walking out a <u>new</u> relationship of Love & respect. This new relationship could NOT be had without the both of us submitting our individual will's to God. <u>**Please believe me**</u>: if my mother & I can Love each other again, there's hope that you & your child(ren)'s love will flourish (abound), also!

But remember from Ingredient/Chapter 7's reference...as a parent you are to *teach* your child(ren) *how* to Love in spite of challenges & connect that abounding-Love to knowledge & discernment. Your child knowing what true Love is & how that Love is *supposed to be* nourished (& grow) **will enable them** to prove what is excellent for their **own** lives. But if quality time is <u>not</u> spent teaching & SHOWING them what true Love is, <u>*how*</u> are *your* off-spring supposed to learn WHAT True Love *is...& is not?* –Telling your child that you love them simply IS

NOT enough. The *devil is* going to *tell your child that he loves them also...* The question is: **who will the child most likely believe...** AND....WHY?

DOUBLE-PARENT HOMES THAT LACK PARENTAL UNITY:

It is moderately possible that some have deceived themselves into believing that because there is a mother & a father in the home (individual, parental roles broken down quite intentionally), that '*things aren't that bad*'. After all, you've been able to 'stay' together, even IF you're staying together is *FOR* the kid(s).

Or maybe the *illusion of unity* is for the two of *you*. Humans have become rather *addicted* to living up to self-created civic-images seeking to satisfy the on-lookers of Life. Yet, it is not the on-lookers that are living the Life of Lies that you've crafted & caressed.

Yes! You were able to 'get' through another family get-together &/or that community function *without*

anyone suspecting that you two (parents) **aren't** uni-
fied, **aren't** speaking to each other & (some) not
even *sleeping* with each other (be it: same room
&/or physically). However, you are riding in the car,
with the witness(es) to **ALLLLL** your public deceit
& are unawaringly **losing all respect from the seed**(s)
that you *claim* that you are staying together *for*.

Very simply realized, if there is **no** order in the
home, *there is chaos* (a.k.a.: disorder). **Things do not**
have to be LOUD in order for chaos to be occurring.
(Selah/Meditate on this.) Most times, chaos/disorder
is prevalent in the places of secret silence. –In the
places of the 'held'-tongues coupled with brute bitterness.

Disorder can be found in every occasion where the
'pink elephant' is adamantly ignored. 'Pretending',
'playing the role', 'going through the motions', 'fak-
ing it till you make it'...no activation of *any* of these
cliches will bring Sustaining Life to the relationships involved in *this* family. Just because the mom
& dad attended the soccer game, this does not make
the child *feel* Love (in & *of* the home).

Thankfully, the Bible gives us the answer for what **order** a home is supposed to own. 1 Corinthians 11:3 (KJV) clearly says, "...*that the head of every man is Christ; & the head of the woman is the man; & the head of Christ is God.*" IF the man, is submitted in his spirit AND his heart to God & God's Word & God's Holy Spirit...& the woman is so submitted to this *same* man & her heart is lined up with his, being a God-chaser her *very* self...everything else will be aligned... because Christ Jesus **already** recognizes, knows & correlatingly **shows** that He is aware that God is the Head of *Himself.* Jesus said NUMEROUS times that He *only* says & does what Our Father (Yahweh) says & does. That sounds like submission to me.

When the man *loves, thinks* & *acts* like God & the woman is submitted to that *same* God-vision (for her Life) & the two of them spiritually warfare to stay **united** on *this* front –to raise & rear their children in the **same**, fearful admiration of God; this will be a power-packing family. *Nothing* will be impossible to them because they all believe...*together.*

But of course... things happen.

It may be the man that is not willing to be emotionally, mentally, financially, physically &/or *spiritually* <u>HONEST</u> OR it may be the female that is walking in this described deceit. This relational tug-of-war marriage will not cease in friction until the chaotic portion/party(ies) is: 1) willing to admit responsibility & 2) to personally & willingly adhere to the family plan of 1 Corinthians 11:3. It HAS to be an *individual, desired* change, NOT changing to 'keep the peace'. Not 'changing' because you don't want to 'look bad'. –You need to desire changing because you genuinely **care** & **Love God's Way**!

There can be many things that the mother & father do not agree on: money handling, frequency of sex, romantic applications, child-rearing, food preparation & intake, household chores, quality time spent with each other, quality time spent individually, extended family, friends, work, co-workers, lack of work, hygiene, weight additions or losses, conversational tactics, lack of communication/understanding, lack of consideration &/or support...the list really could go on. But unless the mother & father are willing to come **together** to rebuild THEMSELVES & their relationship (!), the

child(ren) are *slyly* scheming *(as* **they** *age)* to get
what they want from the parent that is most willing
to bend to *their* immature-parental will.

After all, in these types of marriages (double-parent
homes that lack parental unity) more often than not,
one of the parents is trying to please the child(ren).
Doesn't it help when you feel like <u>you</u> have an ally?
Sadly, the parent that thinks <u>this</u> way doesn't realize that simply giving into the will of the child in
hopes that the child will gratefully obey them 'one-
day'(!), is *actually* **setting themselves up** to be indirectly, **emotionally & financially** *pimped* by their *own*
child(ren) (with the accompanying disregard attached).

I know...that it hurts (the thought of this). But...it is
very true.

Pride is the **TRAP** of this dysfunctional family.
–Pride & fear. Fear of letting go. Fear of admitting
fault. <u>Pride</u> **is the** *<u>fortress</u>* **for fear**. You've felt like
you were beating your head against a brick wall???
You were beating against the *spirit of pride*. Out of
all of the tactics that the enemy uses, *pride* is the
one that is SELF-deceiving (James 1:22).

Pride is an **invisible**, engulfing slime that oozes over one's spirit & *suffocates* Love & Life from *within* the individual. **The spirit of Pride seeks to please** *it-self* **&** **starve** the human-host **of incoming, nurturing Love!**

Pride is *addicted* to **APPEARING to be right; & **doesn't** care if it *actually* IS right. ******

---

*Pride will **not fully** admit fault &/or responsibility.* Pride will *always* find a way to blame others, even in the smallest way. **Pride is a demonic spirit**......We do not wrestle with flesh & blood (Ephesians 6:12). You **will not** win trying to use silent treatments, coaxing &/or appeasement measures.

Yes...he or she did whatever. But what was the reason that the two of you married? Marriage says that for the remaining of your breathing capabilities you want to spend your Life striving with this other person. If you married for any other reason than this, you are definitely going to have to seek quali-

<u>fied</u>, spiritual AND professional, marriage counseling.

But the thing to remember in all of this, is your child(ren)'s soul(s). It's the *unspoken* things that are being *rooted* into your child's spirit. The lack of unity in this marriage is being inadvertently taught to your child's psyche. *Subliminally*, **they learn deceit.** *Subliminally,* **they learn the craftiness of arguing & manipulation.** Subliminally, they learn to 'fake the funk' for people & go back to an earthly hell when returning home. *Subliminally,* **they learn how to disregard the feelings & concern of others in order to get what they want.** Indirectly, they negatively learn how to react (instead of positively respond) when they don't get their way. Why would your children want to talk to *you* when you & your spouse do not want to talk to each *other* (reasonably)? What examples have been appropriately modeled for the child to even *know* what *to* do? You are asking **more** from them than what you are requiring from *yourselves;* & **you** are the heads of the home! Good leaders follow their **<u>OWN</u>** rules.

SUMMARY:

The devil is all about attempting to make God's people lose focus off of the fact that behind ANY & EVERY situation, *regardless* of what it is, **there is a spiritual WAR for souls that is occurring**. While you're working your 'butt off' as a single-parent or while you are spending time alone in 'your' room within a double parent home with no parental unity, the devil is attempting to *spiritually* spew sadistic seeds into your children. The enemy of man, **the devil, is seeking to make your child think that what is abnormal is normal** –so that your child can continue to reproduce abnormalities in *future* relationships –so that generational curses can be created & futuristically transferred *by them*. The devil is always after the next...generation; and the devil will use YOU to get to them.

These two homes are very different. But the enemy's spiritual goal is the same: **get** *the kids...*

Be willing to shift your (spiritual) **perspective to the children.**

Pray to God for your accommodating, spiritual answer. Apply what God says via the Holy Spirit.

Humble your hearts & pray for spiritual, emotional, mental & physical strength <u>&</u> wisdom to *endure, with a RENEWED mind* (Romans 12:1, 2). Get your focus off the surface issues. Realize the enemy is spiritually *after* your *children!* Choose to side with God & war to save your family & future lineage.

INGREDIENT NINE

Immaturity

(mentally, emotionally, spiritually)

Immature is commonly defined as: 1) not fully developed 2) having or showing emotional or intellectual development appropriate to someone **younger**. Dictionary.com defines *immaturity* as: youthful behavior; or lacking wisdom, insight & emotional stability.

Why...would immaturity be an area of spiritual concern? How can immaturity lead you to a devil's **TRAP**?

The state of immaturity denotes that there is a certain level of understanding that should **already** be attained, that the subject has *not yet* acquired. Immaturity suggests that the growth of the subject, in whatever designated area, is *underdeveloped.* In the <u>WAR</u> for <u>SOULS</u>, being immature is similar to being an <u>un</u>informed, directionless, <u>un</u>disciplined, spiritual-kamikaze. –A danger to him/herself, as well as to others.

It is said that finances, more times than not, is the culprit of disintegrated relationships. Some may argue that infidelity may be a worthy opponent for the number one spot. *I suggest*...**that the underlying 'root'** (for both) **is an individual that is mentally, emotionally &/or spiritually immature.**

As in Ingredient/Chapter 8, the spirit of **Pride** *nurtures* & <u>protects</u> immaturity. Pride & immaturity are 'kissing cousins'. The immature mindset & immature outlook is *rarely* willing to admit lack of knowledge or possible inadequacies!!! How detrimental an immature viewpoint can be to any & virtually <u>all</u> **relationships...!**

As we learned or reviewed prior in Ingredient/Chapter 7: ***Settle-Mind-Set***, pruning (the cut-ting away of things in our lives) is *actually* good. Pruning is a necessary action that God uses to make our Lives *eventually* thrive into the purposed Lives He intended for us to walk out. <u>Submitting</u> to the **invisible** action of pruning requires a **mature** mindset & a **mature** heart. –A sincere & genuine TRUST that God, Yahweh Himself, **knows** who & what is best for your Life. Also, a <u>**mature standpoint realizes that being 'wrong' does not devalue an individual**</u>. *And if ANYthing, admitting* to being wrong can *improve* relationships, if the other party(ies) are mature persons *themselves.*

Let's discuss separately the 3 mentioned immaturity types.

MENTAL IMMATURITY:

God created the brain to be the ruler of the human body (systematically). All signals & directives for your body (voluntarily & involuntarily) flow through your brain. Even if there is a portion of your body that does not work as originally intended (by God), the brain still tries/attempts to send signals & commands to the desired areas to accomplish what *it* thinks needs to be achieved.

If a person is mentally immature, this means that someone's thought patterns & observational techniques & assessments are under par. Bluntly stated, their thought-processes are inadequate.
–Insufficient. ***This insufficiency now rules this person because this is the mode*** of *their* **brain**. <u>You cannot expect full potential from this individual when it comes to decision-making</u>. (Please re-read the prior 2 statements.)

Culprits to a mentally-immature person are **ignorance** (lack of knowledge) & again, **pride** (arrogance/lack of humility).

NOTE: there is a stark difference between confidence & arrogance. It takes a trained, spiritual eye to be able to tell the difference between the two.

A mentally-immature person **cannot STAND** to be told that what they are doing, thinking, saying, planning, feeling, wanting, believing, praying &/or hoping is WRONG or can be improved! Based on their restricted recall & deficiency in data, *this in-dividual* can only walk in a limited perception of what can *possibly* be true.

In order to foster a *false sense* of self-esteem, the spirit of pride usually steps in to make the mentally-immature person **falsely** 'feel' good...causing them to act <u>out</u> of character (being mean, rude, loud, haughty, obnoxious, etc.). Pride will cause the men-tally-immature individual to often lash out on oth-ers who threaten to expose that they, *in fact, may* be wrong or inaccurate.

Orrrrr...the spirit of pride will cause the person to operate from the *opposite* side of the spectrum, which is to *completely* shut down internally & allow *anger* to be birthed in their heart (after *pride* & *embarrassment* made love), causing this individual to now view this specific subject negatively. This person usually will <u>avoid</u> the subject of personally-perceived ridicule <u>at all costs</u> & will shut down any attempts at conversation, as the seed of anger ma-tures into bitterness.

These things should not be...

We are called to have the mind of Christ Jesus (1 Corinthians 2:16). Christ Jesus (Himself) learned obedience through the things that *He* suffered (Hebrews 5:8). How is it that Yahweh God, Who put Himself in flesh of Body & became Jesus, The All Powerful, All Mighty, Holy One of All, submitted **His** Power to LEARN how to be the best HUMAN that <u>He</u> could be?...& <u>*we*</u> *do not think* that we need to do the same?! REGARDLESS of age!!!!!

Being mentally-immature will stagnate your Life & cripple <u>ALLLLLLLLLLLL</u> your relationships. You will perpetually make bad decisions for your Life that will cause you to go further & further *down* into a *self*-made pit. This is a **TRAP** because you step onto a rickety, merry-go-round, located in a dried up wilderness, where nothing changes & nothing grows. You will find yourself constantly blaming others for why what <u>*you*</u> think should be...is *not*. And nothing will change until you **<u>mentally</u>** change.

No human can know all things.
It is only God Who is Omniscient (All Knowing). It will take submitting to God's Word & His Nature to break this mentally-immature yoke off of you & cause you to desire to learn all that you can (& to

admit & accept when you are *wrong*). The Bible
says that the wise will listen & **increase** in
knowledge (Proverbs 1:5). If you (we) aren't listening & learning from others (who are ***WORTH*** listening to)...then...that...means...that...we...are
not..........*wise.*

(I know; it hurt me too.)

A powerful scripture to break mental-immaturity:
Proverbs 1:7 "...The fear of The Lord is the beginning of knowledge; fools despise wisdom & disci-
pline." In this scripture, it is easy to tell whether or
not we are playing the part of a fool.

I believe that this SHOULD sum up what we should
learn about why we need to stay from the **TRAP** of
mental-immaturity. Look at learning & gleaning
from others as a positive thing! Learning from what
others do or do *not* do can save *us* & protect *us* in
the **long** run.

God said that He would lead us into all Truth (John
16:13); we must be wise enough to recognize (mentally) what __is__ Truth & what is *selfish*-opinion, **within
ourselves**. When we can successfully & continually

do this *first* with our selves, then it will be easy to recognize when others are not doing the same! It will also be easy to know who we *should* be listening to (Proverbs 12:5) & who we should not be listening to. (Proverbs 1:1)

EMOTIONAL IMMATURITY:

We all know people that express this level of low-grade humanity, even if the example that we have is our very own selves. Having a relationship with a person who is emotionally-immature is tiresome & can wreak havoc on any potential positivity.

An individual that is emotionally-immature has ripened roots that are so full-grown that they choke the Life & newness out of *all* situations & circumstances that can promote health & growth. An emotionally-immature mindset creates an atmosphere similar to quick-sand.

One of the biggest indicators *to whether or not someone is emotionally-immature is whether or not this person can be* <u>*rationally*</u>...**<u>HONEST</u>**...about **<u>their</u>** thoughts, their opinions, &/or their *feelings*. – We are talking about to the degree where this per-

son gets confronted about what is the Truth regarding *their* stance & Truth is <u>not</u> willingly offered
(passive aggression: "Nothing is wrong" –when it
really <u>**IS**</u> something wrong). OR, if it IS offered, it is
done from a *defensive* standpoint, where they *lash*
out, possibly raise their voice unnecessarily & make
accusations –all based on past-influenced, painful
opinions.

There is no relationship that can be had (where
growth & closeness is desired) **that will not require
the two parties to become vulnerable at some standpoint, for the** sake **& the** cause **of resolution.** The
emotionally-immature individual will not be willing
to enter the state of vulnerability for the greater
good of the relationship.

Being emotionally-immature (as an adult) can be
regarded as the equivalency of an adult that has an
upgraded, temper tantrum. Words are heard, but
the *interpretation* is often *misconstrued.* Assump-
tions are made and accepted due to pride/self-
righteousness. Clarity is *not* sought, because this
person thinks that *what <u>they</u> think* is concrete &
there is no possible variance. Being in a relationship

(of **whatever** kind) with a person who is emotionally-immature will always be like an unnecessary tug-of-war, where regardless of strength, there will be no winner, no real resolution & *no advancement.*

Jeremiah 17:9 says that the 'heart is deceitful among all things". This is a very powerful Scripture that indicates that we are to always take our thoughts & feelings to God for Guidance & appropriate action. Just because we *think* a thing & *feel* a certain way does not mean that another aspect is not to be considered. Being emotionally-immature is comparable to having a pillow pressed hard against all things that you want to live & thrive. The *daunting* Truth... is: the emotionally-immature individual is the one that presses the pillow inadvertently unaware.

Can you see how being emotionally-immature is a certain **TRAP**? This type of immaturity is, again, likened to quick sand: the more you move, try, & act —the worse things get. Emotional-immaturity is cloudy vision, misconstrued perception...due to spiritually-inappropriate, unfiltered thoughts.

To break free from the **TRAP** of emotional-immaturity, we have to decide within ourselves, that if we DO want to seek resolve, then we have to be 1) *willing to admit* our concerns TRUTHFULLY & RESPECTFULLY & 2) we have to be OPEN to hear & **consider** that *our original standpoint* was not accurate & that our original standpoint **should not** be held onto (by us). The larger **TRAP**s of pride & fear are the two things that would prevent us from operating in these two manners explained (mentioned in the prior sentence).

SPIRITUAL IMMATURITY:

As of current, there is one scripture that is screaming out within my spirit concerning spiritual-immaturity. This scripture is: "...Be not unequally yoked with unbelievers... (2 Corinthians 6:14)"

Now, many people will teach upon this scripture in reference to: *being closely connected to someone who does not share the same principles in faith* (in Christ Jesus) as you do. But **I dare you** to go *beyond* mere surface of this scripture. When it comes to this scripture commanding that you do not become closely knitted to an unbeliever, it is *my* personal interpretation that **the Bible is suggesting that you do not get tied up with someone who does not believe on your LEVEL/DIMENSION!!**)

There are many WOLVES (male & female) that are 'rocking' sheep firs **IN** THE CHURCH, trying to *'portray'* themselves as being of the *same* faith & of the same belief system. But(!), when you get these same persons off to themselves, 9 times out of 9 they **will** try to suggest or get you to *participate* in some action that is <u>outside</u> of YOUR appropriate level of belief in what God has ALREADY said & proved (in His Word).

It is not enough for someone to tell you that they believe in Christ Jesus; it is not enough that they go to church; it is not enough that they are on 19 ministries; it *is not enough...* that they believe that Jesus is the Son of God & that He is Lord of all. demons (*lower-case intentionally*) know that Jesus Being the Son of God is Truth & factual; so mere admittance of Jesus' Righteous-Standpoint doesn't indicate veracity of a pure heart. (James 2:19)

The Bible ALSO states that **evil behavior corrupts good character/conduct.** (1 Corinthians 15:33) This means that *realistically*, we SHOULD NOT accept, nor anticipate for ourselves to become closely linked with someone that has: ***contrary**-faith potential*, operates in sub-optimal practices (habitually) &/or possesses thought processes that are opposite to the Goodness of God that we are trying to manifest in our own Lives. **We CANNOT expect to be an aid in facilitating change in people who are not <u>persistently</u> seeking or wanting change for** *themselves* (...change that is God's Way).

On repeat mode, **it is not enough** that the person of interest (to you) believes in Christ Jesus...There are ***<u>many</u>*** devils in <u>many</u> Spirit-filled churches, that are *strategically* positioned on: worship teams, usher boards, adjutants/armor bearers, cooks, PR/Marketing reps, music ministries, dance teams, administrative teams, elder/deacon boards, parking lot ministries, the nursery, Christian-Educational departments, the mothers' ministries, Audio/Visual teams, finance committees, even ministers delivering the Word of God **IN** God's pulpit.

Titles, ministry memberships & community service <u>do not</u> indicate holiness & pure motives!!! It is not what one *says* or SHOWS publically that we should have regard for. It is not about the connections, *people!* It is the things that people *do* or SUGGEST (to us or others) behind *'closed'* doors (when they think that no one is looking or that no one will know) that *should* be *the* indication for who is on our faith level/dimension & who, *in fact*, IS NOT.

None of us are or will ever be in a position where we will not face *temptation* (the idea or suggestion to participate in contrary conduct that is opposite of God's Will & Word). For those who have accepted Christ Jesus as their Lord & Savior, **we should be expecting temptation**...why else (...?) did Jesus give us a model prayer in which, when we don't know what to pray, we can *at least* ask that we '...not be lead into temptation & that we would be delivered from evil..' (Matthew 6:13).

Temptations involve Tricks. Tricks involve deception. Deception involves **TRAP**s. Spiritual-Immaturity (not knowing what you **should** know spiritually) is a dangerous, self-engaged noose that only means to harm one's self. The Word of God is our Spiritual Measuring Stick for ALL that we should do & what we should not do in this Life. The Word of God reveals deception in people & in situations. (And the Holy Spirit is The Confirmer; John 16:13)

***Example: We *cannot allow ourselves* to become church-attending whores (male or female), just because someone:
---says that they believe in Jesus, attends church, wears a cross on a T-shirt from time to time, knows some scriptures, talks Kingdom-'lingo' &/or has an affiliation or connection with someone of importance within your church &/or community.

We MUST come UP in our learning the Word of God & **acceptance** of God's Goodness & Truth in our Lives. **Half** of what we tolerate (from the devil) is because, *spiritually*, we have no self-esteem. The lack of spiritual self-esteem **within us** is what *prevents* us from saying **no** to the *inadequacies* that are offered...to *us*... *through* people... that are *under* demonic influences, while wearing spiritual masks & spiritual hats!!!

This is why there are so many relationships in the Kingdom of God where there is no harmony & no balance (spiritually). You thought because he/she came to church with you...that he/she was all **IN**(??!!)....But you didn't *wait* for the evidence of spiritual proof that this individual was *responsible enough for their OWN* Life's (spiritual) decisions. You **did not wait** for proof that they aren't a spiritual, demonic influence in the Lives of you & others. And when God <u>**DID**</u> show you the Truth about who that person *actually is* spiritually (outside of the dream you've conjured up), you CHOSE to *ignore* the Warnings, because of *your* desire...superseding God's Will. (God *help* us, Father!)

Doesn't it matter (to you) if '*they*' only show YOU '*good*', but behind your back they are trying to get away with *whatever* they think can be hidden *from you* & other people? Spiritual-immaturity can cause us to do something that God has NEVER called us to do...which is to *settle*.

Spiritual-immaturity is like having blinders on, unnecessarily. Blinders are intended for animals (like horses) that someone wants to control. Blinders are a pair of small leather screens attached to a horse's bridle to prevent it from seeing sideways & behind (Google Definition). When it comes to humans, blinders are something that prevents someone from gaining a full understanding of a situation (Google Definition). Blinders are something that prevents discernment (a Merriam-Webster Definition). Spiritual-immaturity is like walking around, living *your* Life, making decisions, with your hands over your *own* eyes.

It's equivalent to gambling with your Life, making decisions that are not based on <u>**any**</u> spiritual research OR sound, wise advice. Spiritual-immaturity is likened to literally 'throwing caution to the wind' & '*hoping for the best*'. The Word of God IS how we appropriately 'see' people, places & processes as they REALLY are. Just because we do not 'see' '*it*', doesn't mean that '*it*' isn't so... (whatever **that** may be)

Spiritual-immaturity is a definite **TRAP** because it will always cause you to end up in situations where you *should* be the victor; but your hope that was based on a thought (that had **no** relevance to God's Truth) allowed you to be spiritually duped (swindled). The important thing to realize is that just because we are operating *in* spiritual-immaturity; it <u>does NOT</u> take away responsibility *from us*... the requirement for us to (spiritually) 'grow up'.

The Bible clearly indicates that we are to be studiers of the Word of God. WHY?! So that WE are able to rightly divide & decide what is Truth & what is error. (2 Timothy 2:15) Spiritual-MATURITY will cause us (eventually) to have more good decisions 'under the belt' of our daily lives versus bad decisions. There will be less *'shoulda, coulda, wouldas'*. Why? Because the Word of God in our hearts & minds, coupled with the Advising of the Holy Spirit whispering *in* our spirit & in our ears, will cause us to be people who can **know** what should be done in most, if not all situations. (Daniel 6:3)

Not desiring or not implementing the acquisition of God's Word **in your soul** will make you be behind, *constantly* stumbling around, *continually* 'playing the victim' in your **own** adult life, *not* knowing why...*foolishly* (Proverbs 1:5-7).

In summary, we must tie these three areas of (mental, emotional & spiritual) immaturity together. In the beginning of this Ingredient/Chapter, we discussed that the state of immaturity denotes that there is a certain level of understanding that should **already** be attained, that the person has not yet acquired. Immaturity suggests that the growth of the individual, in whatever designated area, is *underdeveloped.*

The devil, the enemy of man, absolutely prizes immaturity in people. As long as one does not know & does *not* operate in **what is best** (according to God's Word), then this same person will not operate in God's Power! And the devil certainly does not want God's Power (in us) to be used against *him!* The devil KNOWS that Christ Jesus shared with us **His Authority** <u>OVER</u> the works of the devil's wickedness.

The devil <u>*already knows*</u>...that he is (spiritually) 'under our feet' & that **he is subject to what** *we* **spiritually decree.** But as long as people do not know nor operate in their proper, spiritual positions, the devil has free course to continue to negatively influence people mentally, emotionally & spiritually...causing them to be an *unaccommodating* force in their *own* lives & in the lives of people that they are in connection with.

Mental, emotional &/or spiritual-immaturity, individually & collectively, can be a **TRAP**. Immaturity is a **TRAP** of self-imposed blindness; causing one to be haphazardly, driving their **Life** around, with no aim, no structure, no direction & no plan. When we live according to *whim, chance, 'luck', feelings, bitterness, anger, fear*...(instead of taking **Authority** over our minds, emotions & spirits)...we voluntarily become a 'play-thing' for the devil. We MUST be willing to learn God's Word, so that we can learn God's *Way*.

God's Way is the Light for our paths...& The Guide for our decisions that WILL help us...stay OUT of immaturity's **TRAP**s.

The key to unlock it: *higher, spiritual thoughts in agreement with God.* (Isaiah 55: 8-11)

INGREDIENT TEN

What Do You

REALLY...Believe?!

Now, **IN THIS** ingredient/chapter, I know that God is going to cause me to... 'go *in*'. It's all about walking what you've been talking, at *this* point. One of the **biggest** pet peeves of mine is people that do a bunch of talking, but what they *say* cannot be seen in what they *do*. The devil has caused **so many** people to be *self*-deceived that we **cannot** look at mere actions anymore & think that we have people or situations 'pegged out'. (James 1:21-22)

We <u>really</u> have to trust & depend on The Holy Spirit for **Truth**. Someone can attend church *every* Sunday for 20 years & not receive ANY Word in their Spirit that will *last* through a storm or positively change & upgrade their lives & relationships (Matthew 7:24-27). And just because they went to church every Sunday for 20 years, we can **foolishly** believe that that person has 'it all together'.

You see, The Word of God is the *only* Force that will <u>outlast</u> ALL situations. The Bible says that The Word of God is what <u>will</u> stand FOREVER (Isaiah 40:8; 1 Peter 1: 24-25). This is why we are continually admonished in The Word of God, to make Christ Jesus (Who *IS* The Word) our **Foundation**. The Word of God needs to be deposited in our spirits & **hidden** <u>in our hearts</u>, so that The Word of God *cannot* be easily plucked out.

One will never know the strength of something, *until it is tested*. This goes from cars, to tampons, to pampers, to tools, to tamper-proof containers/equipment, to shoes, to active wear, to electronic devices, to safes, to surgical instruments...most everything exchanged or used will qualify for testing.

We, *ourselves*, will be tested to see if we really...**believe**...The Word of God.

As when testing any product, if the content of the product is **not** of quality, the result of the creation will be some sort of fracture or failure. That's why only certain vehicle producers can exclaim 'quality' when they bleed their car advertisements over the minds of people. A certain amount of money has to be spent for producing & testing material that will not only drive well & is cost efficient, but will additionally keep the passengers safe, in even the most extreme, dangerous situations. This is where we'll hear..."ranked in the top 3 of best vehicles for an automobile accident..." (–or something of the like).

Spiritually...we (again) will be tested, as well. And whether or not we'll *last* depends on what type of 'ground' we are. Now, to understand what I am talking about & where God is leading us, you have to read (beforehand & partially understand-at *least*) **Matthew 13: 18-23.**

This is talking about the 4 categories of people that are in the world today.

You & I fit into **ONE** of these four categories. The most important thing to realize is that the category that we fit in is the determining Truth & <u>explanation</u> of our Lives & how you & I are living it currently!

If you are really serious about change in your Life, if you really want to upgrade your spirit, if you really want greater understanding of what's necessary for you, according to what God says, if you REALLY want to stay out of a demonic **TRAP**...please take the time to read/re-read the 6 verses listed in Matthew 13: 18-23, so that we can **all** be on the same page spiritually. We will wait [for everyone's chance] to do so...

....

Ok.

Now that we have all *(believing by faith that you participated in the reading, by re-reading or briefing)* reviewed Matthew 13: 18-23, let's go over each category of person. (For **greater** understanding, it is suggested that you start at verse 1 of Matthew, chapter 13...) Each type of ground reveals what <u>quality of faith</u> each type of person has when it comes to: *hearing, receiving, believing* & MANIFESTING God's Word.

Ground 1---Seeds were sown along the path & the birds came & *devoured* them.

Ground 2---Seeds fell on rocky ground, where there was very little soil & the seeds *immediately* sprang up; but due to lack of soil, when the sun rose (the heat), growth of the seeds were *scorched* by the sun.

Ground 3---Seeds fell among thorns. The thorns grew up & *choked* the seeds.

Ground 4---Seeds fell on good soil & *produced* some grain, some 100-fold, some 60, & some 30.

In **Ground 1**, (explanation found in verse 19 of Matthew 13), this is where someone hears the Word of the Lord God & **does NOT understand it**, then the devil comes & snatches away what was sown in that person's heart.

In **Ground 2**, (explanation found in verses 20 & 21 of Matthew 13), this is where someone hears the Word of God & *immediately* receives it with joy (ex: running around the church / 'shouting' / internally excited); *yet,* this individual **has no root** in his/herself; so they endure *temporarily,* & when tribulation or persecution arises ON **ACCOUNT** OF THE WORD (that **they** received), *immediately* this person falls away.

In **Ground 3**, (explanation found in verse 22 of Matthew 13), this is where someone hears the Word of God, **but the *cares of the world*** (enticements/distractions/trying times) & the *deceitfulness of riches* **choke** the Word of God *within this person* & this person proves to be *unfruitful* when it comes to the Word of God (deceitfulness of riches = the **LOVE** of money---**NOT** money itself, the *inanimate* object---2 Timothy 6:10).

In **Ground 4**, (explanation found in verse 23 of Matthew 13), this is where someone hears the Word of God & they UNDERSTAND it (Proverbs 4:7). *Because* this person understands the Word of God when he/she hears it, their Lives bear (eventual/timely) Fruit as a witness of The Word of God that they've **heard / believed / implemented / executed**...in one case an 100-fold return, in another a 60-fold return & in another example a 30-fold return.

The question remains: what do you ...REALLY... believe?

It's not enough for us to say, " *Yeah. I'm a believer in Christ Jesus. I believe God's Word. God is my All & All. I'm souled & sold out. I cannot go back. The world is this & we are that. There's nothing out there for me anymore. I'm trying to do this 'thing' God's Way...*"

<u>Please note</u>: that each & **every** time, we are in a position to receive God's Word **into** our spirit, the devil is like the tennis ball machine that spits out tennis balls to an individual that needs/wants to practice hitting balls that are being served to themselves. The devil is **ready** to throw <u>any</u> attack, ploy, device, scheme, situation, circumstance, distraction, deception, frustration, rumor, temptation, misunderstanding...to get us side-tracked & focused on *whatever* the devil 'threw' at us, **instead** ...of focusing, believing & concentrating on what <u>God</u> *said*.

In the book of James (in The Holy Bible), James strongly suggested that we are not to be hearers of the Word of God only; that we are also to be DOERS of the Word. (James 1:22-27) James goes on

further to explain that if we find that we are someone who *only* hears the Word of God & discover
that when it comes to our personal Lives, that we
are not, *in fact*, doers/**implementers** of God's Word,
then we are DECEIVING *ourselves*. This is a very
notable Truth that needs a blaring horn & a glar-
ing, red, flashing light attached to it.

→ You see, the devil can only set up a **TRAP** for us
by him being an avid studier of what **we** tend to do (individually). The devil is **very** strategic in all of his
affairs (literally & figuratively). The devil knows
simply by watching our conduct & our *tendencies*
whether or not the Word of God is *actually* 'taking'
root **in** us. The devil can tell by watching our daily
lives & by analyzing our personal, secret decisions,
what type of Spiritual Ground we REALLY are (not
the type of spiritual Ground we *pretend* to be for
others).

To be frank, I must admit that I *personally*, was the
3rd Ground for many years. I was a hearer of the
Word of God **more** than I was a doer of God's Word
(James 1:22). And to give myself SOME credit (no;
pride is *not* stepping in), it wasn't that I let completely go of faith when trials came or that I fell

away altogether from faith in God's Word; but there was <u>not a root</u> of the Word of God in me that would **influence** my actions to become a part of my heart.

*What is she **talking** about*???
–I was RELIGIOUS. **I did** believe God's Word. But I also thought that to SOME degree that I could 'do what I wanted to do'; when I felt like *doing* it, for *whatever* reason I decided was good enough for me to do so. THEN, I thought that when I needed something or quite specifically, if I *wanted* something from God, that I could try to strike a '**deal**' with God, or do 'good' for a *certain* length of time & SURELY that would 'qualify' me to get the 'blessing' that I wanted from God.

I had a '**form** of Godliness' (2 Timothy 3: 2-5), but my Life showed *no* personal, **direct PROOF** of God's Power. –From *God?* **Yes**; there was Proof in my Life of **God's** Power. Was there Proof in my Life of *me... working* <u>God's Power?</u> –Not so much.

And therefore...the **circle** ensued...
What *circle*?! –the **wilderness**.
–The place no one likes to think about.
–The place that people like to live in *denial* & think

that *that* was just what the Israelites went through after being delivered by Yahweh God, from Egypt.

–The place that we OFTEN do not like to take *personal responsibility* for; when it comes to **why** certain things have not changed in *our* lives.

–The place that we do not want to believe that we are *in* because we want to rush to the Promise Land.

–The **wilderness**, which we often get stuck in *longer* than necessary; *due to personal* decisions, complaints, secret beliefs, crooked spiritual-hearts, religious-living & lack of faith.

It was not until I finally BROKE... that God set me free.

Father God, being the Gentle Spirit that He is, AL-LOWED me to operate in the Power that He gave ALL of us, which is the **Power of Choice**.

Yahweh God gave me two choices: His Way or *not* His Way (which, the latter, will always be connected to the devil). And *then*, even gave me (us) the **Answer** *before* the test(s) & said that I (we) should choose

God's Way, which *is* Life. (Deuteronomy 30: 19, 20)
But *time* after time, *year* after year, that turned into
decades...I'd 'sneak' & do things...**my** way.

Every new situation & new opportunity was a test. –
A test of ME!!!
God was testing to see **what** my heart was made of.
Was my heart made of *His Word* or was it made of
my selfish, lustful, fearful desires? –And every time that
I **CHOSE** to fail...my Life would go back... *around*
again...'replay-central'... to face the same test (Godly
Principle)...in a *different* circumstance...HENCE...*the
circle.*

This one particular, last choice that I made **outside**
of God's Will, that resulted in 'blowing up in my
face';
–hurt me **so** bad that it literally shattered my *reality*
(in every sense of the word). **It completely broke me
to the core of my soul.** And I walked around in a
broken state for 3+ years (Trés años!).

There is *__nothing__* that can describe that pain. There
is nothing that can describe that hurt. There is
nothing that can express how it felt to go through
all of that **ALONE** & have no one that could help

you through it. The pain was SO great; that once
God started restructuring me (since the pieces of
me were **too** shattered for reassembly) I knew...I had
to do it *His Way*...the *next* time.

And that's all that God wanted ANY way.
The Word of God says that God desires a broken
spirit & a contrite heart (Psalm 51:17). Whenever I
read or heard *this* Scripture, I used to think that,
that was so cruel of God. 'Why you want people to
be broken, God (?)', is what I would wonder –not directly asking Him. And then this *last* situation occurred, which brought about *self-reflection*; and I
realized WHY a broken & contrite heart would be
something that God would desire.

It's because of the will of man.

God gave us His Word for Guidance & Protection. –
**But just like with Adam & Eve, God gave *us* the
Power of Choice**. Why? –Because God doesn't want
people with a robotic, uncontrolled, programmed
nature. God desires a people that believe, *obey*, re-
vere/respect & Love Him *from a* Power Position of
Choice.

As long as we are **FULL** of 'self' & are willing to DISREGARD what God says... *in order to do, have & get* what **we** want, then there is nothing that God will do...except, *allow* our Lives to *reap* the repercussions of *our* decisions. <u>Then</u>, allow our failures to make our Lives **circle back** to a position where we will face the *same* test... in a *different* way...AGAIN! (...going in circles, until we *<u>finally</u>* <u>choose</u> obedience unto Yahweh God)

When our spirit, nature, personal will &/or heart becomes (truly) broken, we submit (for real) & internally say:

"Ok God. I *cannot* do this anymore. The pain is too great. I have to be honest with myself; I only sought to please You, so that I could please myself; hoping that You, oh God, would be appeased & give me what I want. I cannot do *this* anymore; it's **not** worth the hurt; it is not worth the angst. It's not worth the back-track; please help me; please help me, Lord Jesus. I need You. I don't know what to do without You. I *cannot* make it without You. Help me, Jesus...please..."

And *then*, we become the vessel that is NOW pliable *enough* for God to shape & mold & form into what **He** designed us to be from **before** the beginning of Time.

It's just like breaking a wild horse; they will buck & buck & buck. But until their WILL breaks--- (their will for personal freedom), there is nothing that you can do with that horse. When our will becomes (finally) broken, **this** is when God can use us & we can now be good Ground for His Word & His Work.

....

Something that is noticeable to me is that when the Bible talked about the four different types of Spiritual Ground that people *can be*...when it described the fourth Ground (which is good-Ground)...this was the only Ground where **what** the enemy of man (the devil) **did** to come up against & attack reception of God's Word in *that* individual... was **NOT** EVEN MENTIONED (!!!).

In the first 3 types of Spiritual Ground, the Bible *plainly* specifies HOW the enemy was able to overcome that particular person who hears the Word of God according to where they are *spiritually*. We were offered a thorough explanation of *how* the devil snatched away the seed of God's Word from that person/Ground. But the individual that hears the Word of God & 1) strives with all diligence to *not only* believe God's Word, but 2) to also hide it in their heart (...to be a Spiritual-Reservoir in tumultuous trials) ANDDDDDDDD, 3) to implement God's Truth *whenever* & *however* possible....*Jesus didn't even take the time* to comment or *hint on* any adversity that the good-spiritual Ground would face (!).

It **has** to be **obvious** that the good-Ground would **ALSO** face hard-ship when it comes to spiritual-assaults; due to the devil not wanting a *real* deposit of God's nature inside of our spirits & souls. But I presume, that Jesus decided that the end result (the bearing of Fruit of God's Word in one's Life) was worth mentioning & was the most important difference & topic for discussion.

Spiritual assaults are to be EXPECTED for anyone who is deciding to TRULY live a Life **of** Christ *(not just for Christ)*. God's Plan is that we *not only believe His Word*, but again, we personally IMPLEMENT

God's Word & God's Will into our Lives. But note: if there is not a <u>TRUE</u> root of God's Word in your Life, the devil will attack & you will not be strong enough to *outlast* the assailment(s) (Proverbs 24:10). You will cower & eventually you will be (in some way) defeated & *eventually* destroyed (John 10:10).

....

What you REALLY believe is important, *not* because of some sort of spiritual, popularity contest; but it is important because what you REALLY believe *can save your* LIFE! What you believe in (truly) is what you, *ultimately*, build your LIFE *on*. The question is: are we a **wise** builder or are we a *foolish* builder? According to Matthew 13, <u>there's a 75% chance that someone is a foolish Life-builder</u>. (Smh) Only 1 in 4 people will have the Godly-Wisdom to <u>actually</u> **do** what God's Word says & 'get it right'. To 'bring it *home*'...how many people are around you in various venues? Count every four people....Only 1 of those four are the odds that someone is *actually*, internally implementing what God is saying & has already said to do. This *does*...include *yourself*...

In Matthew 7:24-27, we have a great lesson that is relational to how we can build our Lives on what God says, (to be our Strong Foundation); <u>or</u> we can build our Lives on '*if*-y' surfaces/suggestions, that promise <u>no</u> guarantee of security when hard times appear...

(Matthew 7:24-27):

" *Therefore, everyone who hears these words of mine & puts them into practice is like a wise man who built his house on the rock. The rain came down, the streams rose & the winds blew & beat against that house; yet <u>it did not fall</u>, because it had its foundation on the rock. But, everyone who hears these words of mine & does not put them into practice is like a foolish man who built his house on sand. The rain came down, the streams rose & the winds blew & beat against that house & it fell with a great crash...*"

How many of our decisions in Life have resulted in a 'great crash'? How many times have we fought condemnation & **regret** because of our involvement in things that we **knew** (quite *specifically*) were 'anti-God'? Making poor decisions every now & again

isn't good necessarily, but I'm not sure if that instantly qualifies us as being a fool. I believe that
means that the choices/decisions we chose were
foolish.

But...when we *habitually*/*repeatedly* make poor decisions (primarily due to not seeking God for Wise
Counsel &/or due to **ignoring** the Holy Spirit), we
can then classify ourselves as **voluntary-fools.** It's
not a nice thought about one's self; but it is very
true.

****

God didn't create us to be fools.
Life can start us *on* that path (nur-
ture/environment), but as adults, we don't have to
stay with a foolish mindset! When we hear the
Word of God & God sends people in our Lives to act
as wise advisors & we choose to throw the '*I'm
grown*' card down & do what we want regardless
(due to pride, immaturity &/or ignorance) ...we enter into the way of a fool...**voluntarily.**

****

Actions **prove** what we believe!
If we hear the Word of God & we <u>do not</u> then...start

taking *personal* measures to bring about an overhaul in the areas of *our* Lives that need a new out-look (via spiritual renovation), then this means simply that **we aren't convinced about what The Word of God says.** If we aren't convinced, we do not believe. If we do not believe in what God says, the devil *will* recognize this & will set up target practice on the hearer of God's Word that *refuses* to be a *doer* of God's Word.

****

Did you know... that you will **never** be able to please God unless you (1ˢᵗ) GENUINELY possess **True** faith *in your heart*?! (Hebrews 11) It is somewhat easy to fool *people*; but we can **never** fool God when it comes to our heart (nor our mind). God sees all things & knows all things. God knows whether or not we really believe His Word! Do not allow *religion* (church acts with no Power & no Holy Spirit-led Purpose) to trick you.

Religion is traditional acts of man-kind, with no Holy Ghost-Spiritual-Transformational-Power. It doesn't matter how many ministries you are on, how many services you attend, how many foundations you start or sponsor nor how much money you sow. If you do not <u>really</u> believe God's Word, *Life* (...the faith-tester) will leave you broken, if not eventually destroyed.

With our Father God, it's *not* about religious acts, robes, sconces, nor rituals; it's about a *personal* **re-lationship with God**. We cannot say that we have a relationship with Yahweh God if we do not believe in His Word! We *cannot say we* have a relationship with God & we *think* that *we* have *no* responsibility to **obey** His New Covenant edicts! And we cannot say that we believe in The Word of The Lord Christ Jesus if our Lives show **no proof** of what *we* believe. Faith *without* works <u>is</u> dead. (James 2: 14-26)

We are not talking about acts that you do/perform publicly. We are talking about your Life that is **not** public.

–The Life that you live when no one is around you.

–The decisions that you make when it seems like no one will/can find out. <u>This</u> is the testing to see *which* GROUND you are when it comes to the seed of God's Word *entering* our Lives.

There was a situation that occurred when someone
that I am really close to had a child that was (according to the doctors) near death due to health complica-
tions. I rushed to the hospital where this loved one
& child were. Immediately, once I entered the
child's hospital room, I began to pray. I laid hands
on the child's body in various areas & just decreed
(even in spiritual tongues) that the child should live
only (!) & not die. –That the child is a descendant of
God. And that God's people **shall** be saved. That
Christ Jesus ABOLISHED death (get ready '*reli-
gious*-ones': ...to *believe* that Jesus' Blood *only* abolishes
eternal death **means** <u>that you do not believe</u> that God's
Blood is **All** Powerful & that <u>you do not believe</u> that God
is TRULY Almighty; how can He be Almighty, yet have
limits?).

The entire time spent in the hospital, the doctors &
machine reports were very bleak. Bottom line: they
gave the report that the family should strive to see
the child one last time; that in the event that there
was not some sort of increased, significant response
from the child, then it would be 'necessary' to consider the child brain-dead. And that consideration
of 'pulling the plug' needed to be contemplated.

In the course of the 72 hour wait, loved ones circulated by the child's bed. One of the parents was crying & talking to me & asked me what *they* should do. WOOOOOOOO! Talk about a spiritual trial!!! I *saw* with my eyes the conditions, the reports, the test results, etc. All the Word that I had stored in me, I couldn't think of ONE scripture to 'pull out' that would be conducive to the situation that we were in. '*By His stripes we are healed*'...didn't seem like 'enough' when you are looking at death looming over the Life of a child. (← I may be too transparent for you)

This is what I told the parent, "*I know what the doctors are saying. I know what the machines are saying. I know what we are seeing. But ALL I KNOW...is that we can <u>NOT</u> count God out.... We cannot give up hope; because God is <u>still</u> Alive.*"

And you guys??? That was **all** that I had.

Anybody that knows me & knows (both) my Apostles (Clark) KNOWS that we get the STRONG meat of God's Rhema (fresh downloaded) Word. But that was all I *had* in *that* situation. No eloquence of speech. No beautiful prayer(s). I was *left* with *raw* faith. –Mere, pure beseeching of God. Just the compilation of raw remembrance, recalling, & reciting of what God said WE *should* believe in, -in my spirit *equaled*: "All I KNOW...is that we can NOT count God out..."

***And after 3 days, the last part of the 3rd day...just like *Lazarus* in the Bible, the child's spirit (God's Life) began to take over!!! (**Hallelujah**!) The child started having vital signs that showed that the body was trying to be an active support *with* the machines, vs the machines doing <u>all</u> of the work for the body. And worthy of mentioning, God prevailed!!! God **made all of those doctors & machines out to be liars!!!** And *in less than one year*, that same child had a complete recovery & was outside playing with their siblings like never before!!!

WHAT DO YOU...*REALLYYYYYYYYYY*....BELIEVE??!!!!!!!!!!

This is what God wants to know about ALLLLL of us. This is what Life-tests come to prove *about* us! Will we believe His Word DESPITE what we are *told*, despite what we *see*, despite what we <u>*feel*</u>, despite what we _know_, despite what we _heard_???! We are talking about the kind of faith that the 3 Hebrew boys (Shadrach, Meshach & Abednego) had.

These 3 Hebrew men were **more** than confident when THREATENED with being thrown into the fiery furnace. They were even so **bold** (_gangsta!_) in their HEART RELATIONSHIP with GOD's WORD & God's Ability...that they told the king Nebuchadnezzar that "..._even if God DOES **NOT** deliver us, we KNOW that He is MORE than able to do so...AND...we will NOT serve/worship your gods_". And after being thrown into the fiery furnace, God **amazingly** used _their_ faith <u>in</u> HIM, to **defy** the odds (the natural laws of earth) & produce 3 miracles simultaneously, which still brings God GREAT Glory today!!! (Daniel 3: 4-30)

God..._cares_...about...us...having...**true** _faith...in...Him...which_...is...faith...in His **Word.**

God, through His Graciousness, Love & Compassion for us, will have people come across our path that will offer wise counsel & advice on what we should do when it comes to believing God's Word & <u>acting on</u> what we believe (Hebrews 13:2, 7,17). **But it is so** very important that we realize that no one can live this faith-walk/journey *for* us!!! Eventually we are going to have to 'walk...what we talk'.

→*For babes in Christ Jesus,* any mentor or spiritual guide that God has raised up in your Life to be a teacher of God's Will is **wonderful** for you to have; but *eventually* (**sooner** than later), you are going to have to grab your OWN spiritual Life by the reigns & dig/dive DEEP into God's Word (continually)...so that you can know what God **sounds** like (for yourself!). It is important *for you to know* what the Holy Spirit sounds like when He corrects & guides you (John 16:13).

The Word of God is the Measuring Stick for The Voice, Thought, and Suggestion that is ACTUALLY *from* God. If you do not know what God's Word says, you will **not** know God's Will & you will **always** be susceptible to be *tricked* into a **TRAP** by the devil. In case you didn't know... the devil KNOWS GOD's WORD (James 2:19)!!! This is how the devil knows whether or not YOU know The Word of God...

Your faith has to be activated **with** the Word of God so that you can institute Godly-actions. We are not talking about playing 'memory game' with the Word of God! <u>**We are not**</u> **talking about reading the Bible in a year!!** We are talking about using your faith to be mixed <u>in</u> *with* God's Word so that when the devil comes (through people, places, situations & circumstances) we won't be deceived *into* a *lesser* thought (Isaiah 55:9).

Eve, in Genesis, was able to be deceived by the devil **because God's Word was in her mind** <u>**only**</u>; *what God said was <u>not</u> in her heart.* Eve *memorized* what God said, but it did not take root in her. So *this* is why what God said was easily removed from Eve's mind by the devil's alternative, manipulative-implications; the devil was able to sway her because her heart was *not* connected to God's Word!!! She only had head-knowledge of what God said.

Eve mentally knew how to 'act', but her <u>**heart**</u> didn't have <u>**relationship**</u> with God. We know this because if her heart had relationship with God, then Eve would have TRUSTED what God *said*. If Eve's <u>**heart**</u> had <u>**relationship**</u> with <u>**God's Word**</u>, Eve would have taken what the devil told her TO GOD & asked ***God*** about it. Due to Eve being a hearer of God's Word <u>only</u>, she denied herself an opportunity for wise counsel (thru going **back** to God with the devil's allegations) & Eve chose/allowed *doubt* to destroy her position with God & then selfishly ...asked her husband to do the same thing.

We've all done it before.
We had a doubtful suggestion presented to us (internally or externally) & we either 1) *didn't* know what God's Position on it was or 2) we ignored God's Position on what we *should* do &/or 3) we *doubted* God's Position due to <u>lack</u> of heart-relationship with God's Word. So, due to ignorance, we chose doubt & went our <u>own</u> way (not God's Way) & walked *eventually* into a demonic **TRAP**.

....

Doubt is like an invisible spider-web that is encasing, like a large room. Initially, doubt is wide open, so that you will not see the sticky-web fibers that are waiting to ensnare you. It's only after we walk <u>into</u> the area of ***doubt*** & *stay there a while*, choosing to <u>close the door by making a decision that is *con-trary* to what God said</u>; **then** the spider-web-like encasement of *doubt slowly...spiritually...* draws *in* on us.

This **TRAP** is very subtle & can take years before one realizes that they are now wrapped in a web & that the first part of John 10:10 is about to happen to them; EVEN if they don't know what John 10:10 says...

I realize that the media has left a heavy impression on people to *believe* that Life is about impressing people, about caring about what others think & about prompting interest in people FOR *you*. But what <u>really</u> matters at the end of **every** day (especially man-kind's upcoming, *Judgment* Day) is what **God** said AND we Living our Lives like we *believe* ...what God said. Whether or not we believe God's Word: *this will not exempt Life from testing us <u>on</u> our belief*(s); to see which type of Ground we... **<u>really</u>** ...are.

This is a part of God's Plan & denial of His Existence or Sovereignty will <u>not</u> change this. You will *not* be excluded due to your <u>chosen</u>-lack of faith-lack-of-participation in God's Divine/Holy Plan! Tests, trials, adversities, struggles, heartache, pain, doubt, fear, anger **will** come & beat on our spiritual houses.

What WE decide to make our Foundation is what will determine whether or not we 'win' through these times.

No... more... pretending.
God <u>knows</u> whether or not we believe His Word!!! Quit trying to impress your pastors & peers. We sure enough cannot believe God's Word if we do not **personally know** what His Word **says** (...because WE read it; *not* from what someone told/tells us).

Let us learn from Eve, <u>not</u> continue to *mimic* her. Let us discover God's heart IN His Word, so that we can connect our heart TO His Heart/His Word. –So that our belief in God's Word will be <u>real</u>; *not circumstantial.*

These are the ONLY ways...that we will prove ourselves ***spiritually worthy*** & stay out of....the devil's webby, doubt-filled, death-**TRAP.**

INGREDIENT ELEVEN

I don't know of many, if *any*, recipes that will instruct you to compile ingredients for an eventual result & NOT ask you to **stir** the ingredients *together*. This being said, we have to realize that there is a generalized <u>formula</u> that the devil is following (through **extreme**, spiritual observation of **each** of us, *individually*)... -when it comes to targeting the Lives of God's people for mass, **spiritual** destruction.

One thing that hasn't been mentioned thus far is that one of the devil's *favorite* lures for us (as God's People) is *pleasure* (a.k.a. **hedonism**). The devil aims to entice us with lust (which **does not only** pertain to sexuality; lust is **anything** that we desire **more** than God).

Once the devil has us positioned, through us taking the *lust*-bait; *now* he has us in an 'unaware' stance where he can open & pour his cans of **bombardment & confusion** on top of us. This will spiritually result in us being stunned & probably spiritually immobile. At *this* point, the devil sequentially spews spiritually-sadist seeds into our Lives in aims of making us dull to operating in our God-given Power & Nature. **Through our** spiritual-ignorance, **the devil turns us into what** *he* **wants us to be.**

Depending on what demonic, spiritual recipe the devil is using, he may not use all 10 of the ingredients that we've covered up until now. The devil may just want to turn us into a spiritual-pancake; so he'll **only** use *Rejection*, with a little *Abandonment* drizzled on top. OR, maybe the devil wants to whip *us* into a spiritual-soufflé by combining *Insecurity*, *Immaturity* & *Ignorance* into our Lives, baked & glazed over with *Low-Self-Worth* & *Low-Self-Confidence*. ORRRRR, maybe the devil wants to turn us into a spiritual-dessert called '*Rocky Road*

Supreme'...& he'll throw/add/mix all ten, mentioned ingredients together & sprinkle **bitterness, unforgiveness & pride** on top (of us) BEFORE... sticking us in a spiritual-freezer (through **our** permission/ignorance), & leave us there...to become *cold* & *hard*.

....

The 'stirring' represents the **negative:** thoughts, seeds, imaginations, occurrences, beliefs, desires, memories, fears, experiences &/or nightmares that are rolling around in your spirit.
–The *circles*; **the shifting from one thought to another with no mental-rest, in repeat-fashion;** thoughts with no *Appropriate*, Straight-lined, Spiritual direction.
–The *chase*, **the demonic, spiritual-pursuit that leaves you physically tired & emotionally & mentally exhausted with no '*determined*' culprit.**

The devil has you in a spiritual whirl-wind that is negatively affecting you & all that pertains to YOU (& your lineage): *mentally, spiritually, emotionally, physically, financially &/or socially.* **And know this:** GOD is <u>not</u> settled with you (us) **not** *knowing* the source of this spiritual-*unrest*; the source of these generational curses that YOU'VE (we've) become the *gateway* to...

It will be **ONLY** when we *wake* to the devices, schemes, plots, plans, worries, stories, ideas & ploys of the wicked enemy of man (the devil), that we will *even* BEGIN to have a chance to fight against these **TRAP**s. It will only be God's Word that will create a transformed mind *in* us that will cause us to undo & **REJECT** the recipe(s) AND the ingredients that the devil keeps trying to pour on top of our spirits. (Romans 12: 1, 2)

We have to start taking spiritual control over our *own* Lives.

We <u>are no longer victims</u>, now... that we are no longer children. We *cannot* change what happened to us or where we grew up or who did or did not raise us, who did or did not protect us, who did or did not harm us, who did or did not neglect us, who did or did not 'participate' in our child-rearing, who did or did not abuse us, who did or did not *believe in* us, who did or did not *include* us, who did or did not properly instruct us, who did or did not *desire* us, who did or did not VALIDATE us. We cannot change any of these things. **The only THING that we have control over is our <u>current</u> selves!!!** –Our *own* thoughts, perceptions & actions (2 Corinthians 10: 3-6). This **is what we must rule over**... WITH The Holy Spirit's Guidance, Instruction & Influence.

God's Word, <u>NOT feelings</u> / <u>NOT emotions</u>, has to be our filter *now*!!!!!

God's Truth has to be our *Measuring* Stick, our *Spiritual* Barometer & our *Reference* Guide for presented situations & circumstances. It's not about what '*they*' said/suggested/did anymore. It's about what GOD said (says) & about what God WANTS!!! Nothing *else* matters; **not** even what *we* think *or* feel (if it's contrary to God's Word, Will & Ways).

How long will we actively/ignorantly **<u>allow</u>** the devil to emit his foreign, spiritual contaminants into our Lives & into our thinking; making us spiritual,

'door-keepers' of access...*FOR the devil*...<u>to</u> our
Lives & to future generations connected to *our* Existence?

Any real cook/chef knows that someone can *provide* a recipe & then **the chef** can choose what they will ADD or take away from the recipe to get the desired result that THEY choose! All day, every day, the devil is offering US suggestions about what *he* thinks would 'taste' good for our situations. We have to stop listening to the illegitimate one (the devil & his spiritual cohorts & puppets); and begin to listen to & **adhere to** the Wisdom & Counsel of The Holy Spirit *through* God's Word!!!!!

It's all about taking charge.
It's all about knowing **Who** God is & who you (we) are <u>in</u> God. It's all about knowing God's Purpose & Plan. It's about <u>knowing</u> God's Word & His Will. **It's about knowing what is good for your <u>spirit</u> & for your <u>Life</u>!**

If you are allergic to peanuts, *surely* –you will *not* be looking for, nor accepting a recipe for peanut butter cookies. *Why would you put your health/Life in danger like that?* **The same goes spiritually!!!** If you (we) know/sense/discern that what is being present-ed to us is a *potential* danger &/or threat **to our SPIRITUAL well-being**, <u>NO</u> amount of 'icing, whipped cream or syrup' will lessen the spiritual-**sting** that the devil **intends** on attacking *our* Lives with!

....

Reflecting back on Ingredient/Chapter 10...it is all about what ...<u>we</u>... believe.

* Do we NOT think that the devil is subjected (con-demned) to <u>**only**</u> being a negative *influence* on man-kind (2 Corinthians 2:13-15)?

* Do we **not** take the devil's *manipulative*-spiritual-*influence* seriously (...that he enacts <u>**through**</u> PEOPLE)?

* Do we <u>**not**</u> realize that *because* of Jesus' Blood that the devil's power is SECONDARY to the Power that Christ Jesus died for **man-kind** to *have & share*

with God?!
(Philippians 2:5, 6)

* Do we **not** think that God's Word is <u>very necessary</u>
when it comes to transforming *our* way of thinking;
so that we <u>won't</u> be the *lackadaisical-Lucy & Lewis*
that will fall prey to whatever 'feel-good' moment
(*hedonism*) is presented to us???

....

God is asking us, "...**WHAT** (??!!) will it *take*, to become *convinced* of My Word?" How many situations
have to enter our Lives in an attempt to **break** our
hardheaded-rebellious-will? How many **YEARS** do
we have to walk around in the circles of chaos &
confusion...**because we continue**...to make decisions...that are **contrary** to God's Word, His Will &
His Ways? What *earthly* or *spiritual* occurrence has
to take place before you (we) will **believe** that God's
Word, Jesus' Blood & The Holy Spirit's Power is
Righteous & True & <u>***more than deserving***</u>... of us to
be Living-sacrifices *for* God's Kingdom?

How long will we allow **hedonism** (*self*-seeking
pleasures, lust, and greed) to make us push God to

the 'backburner' of our Lives, while we become inadvertent, ignorant, **idol-worshippers** (...of ourselves, desires, things & others)? How _long_ will we treat God like He is some genie in a bottle that we can 'strike a deal' with when we get into _hard_, trying, tumultuous times? ONLYYYYY, to go back on what we told God _we_ would **do** if He '_fixed_' ...'it'...

A creator always will test his/her product for authenticity & durability. The rejects...will be discarded. We are the Products of the All-Mighty-Creator, _Yahweh God_. We will not be exempt from being **spiritually**-TESTED to see if we are **true** Lovers of Christ Jesus, or if we are..._convenient, circumstantial-Christian_-counterfeits: _thinking, saying & doing what WE want_, with our hands stuck out, while having our BACKS _adamantly_ turned towards God.

We are in the hour of time where spiritual-answers to the aforementioned questions are being revealed. We are actually living/walking/manifesting the prophesy of _Revelation_, the last, _documented_ book (as of current) of The Holy Bible. Whatever you say that **you believe** WILL be tried to the _ultimate_ degree in the upcoming days, should you live to experience them.

What you believe *matters.*
What **you** ...*believe...* matters. Living what we believe is of the utmost importance. Talk with no 'walk' (talk/belief with no evidence) will make us **UN-qualifiable** for spiritual-endurance. Only Ground #4 had the spiritual soil that was '*good*' enough to be a **proper environment** for the seed of God's **Truth** to take root & **outlast** the 'heat' of the sun, the harsh weather conditions & the elements that Life *presented.*

Do you believe that you are just a victim & that you don't have control over what is produced in *your* Life –through *your* actions/decisions? Do you think that these **TRAP**s are malarkey & merely are topics that you do <u>not</u> have to take seriously??? Can't you reflect on **_your_** Life, your parent's Lives & the generation before them & recognize the demonic, spiritual-mixing-bowl that *everyone* had *their* turn in? **You don't see the similarities**??!!! You don't see the repetition of negative cycles? Don't <u>*you*</u> want change, healing & **True** release?

Change, healing & TRUE release will *only* come...
from your TRUE belief in Yahweh God's Holy
Word. As stated before, this is **not** about some spiritual popularity contest! This is not about who can
'shout' the longest or the *cutest*, nor is it about how
many services you attend in a month; NOR, is it
about how you '*feel*' today! **This is about whether or
not we have true faith in what God's Word says**; a
faith that will come *out* as proven fruit, AFTER the
seasons of storms & rains come to TEST those
things that *we* say that **we** believe in.

1 Peter 5:8 says that we should be sober-minded,
because the devil walks around like a roaring lion
(trying to spiritually intimidate you/us) looking for
someone to devour. Relationally, this means that the
devil is **looking** for someone who is *spiritually ignorant* &/or *spiritually weak*, that he can lure into a
spiritual **TRAP** & *stirrrr*...that individual into one
of his demonic, spiritually-binding recipes.

....

The devil is called the 'angel of light'. The devil
knows how to disguise himself & make himself appear *beautiful* & *dreamy*. The devil is an avid studier of human-desires. he (intentionally lower-cased)

knows what we/humans like because he has studied man-kind **ever since** God *created* man-kind. And unlike MOST people...the devil <u>**KNOWS**</u>...the Word of God!!!

The devil **KNOWS** God's Will. The devil **KNOWS** that his own power is inferior to God's Power!!! The devil **KNOWS** that God made Himself *into* Jesus so that He could reconcile man-kind *unto* Himself through offering <u>*His Holy Self*</u> as THE One-Time <u>*Sacrifice*</u> for sins of <u>all</u> that would *believe, accept* God's Truth & *Live* according to God's Word. **The devil KNOWS that GOD has shared** *His* **Holy Power with man-kind & that** <u>**man-kind is SUPERIOR to the devil**</u>, *through* the *Work* of Christ Jesus.

The devil can only be successful in the lives of people who <u>choose not</u> **to take** *ownership* **of their lives** *spiritually.* The devil can only be successful in the lives of <u>people who choose</u> to ignore God's Word & **think** that *their own* desires & plans for living... SUPERCEDE God's Will, Purpose & His Word.

As explained earlier, *this* way of thinking (choosing **your** wants **over** God's Will) is <u>**hedonism**</u>. Hedonism is the entry for the devil's demonic **TRAP**s that have *invisible, spiritual tentacles* reaching out to *spiritually*: *manipulate, trick, control & overtake* YOU & *eventually* your children & *everyone* connected to your life/lineage.

"...this is JUST how I am..." will **not** save you.

Doing as Romans 12: 1, 2 suggests will make you a worthy, spiritual conqueror. When we have a transformed mind, a higher-self-value & a strong BE-LIEF Foundation (in The Word of God), we are in the proper position to spiritually-'*see*' & '*smell*' what the devil is trying to 'cook up'. Spiritually, we are alerted to the devil's **TRAP**s/recipes (John 16:13). *Deciding* to embrace God's Word as Truth will cause you (us) to set up spiritual (& natural) **STANDARDS** in our Lives that will cause us to STOP voluntarily submitting **our God-given Power** to the devil (THROUGH PEOPLE), so that he will **no longer** be able to *spiritually*: lie to us, bind us & work to *eventually* destroy us from the inside out! (John 10: 9, 10)

If you chose to ignore Wisdom & ignore the Word of God, you are like Clark Kent (*Superman's* human disguise) eating chocolate cake with strawberries & kryptonite-icing on top. ***Feel-good* moments** with the devil <u>are</u> & can ONLY be temporary! The only long-lasting thing that the devil can HONESTLY offer you/us is **destruction** (although the devil will *never* tell you/us the truth **voluntarily**).

Everything that is connected to destruction, the devil will **always** hide from us. The devil will **always** attempt to present a desirable, ***believable*** version of himself. The devil wants you/us comfortable & re-laxed while he wraps a spiritual noose around (y)our neck. The devil doesn't like *opposition*; which is why he offers **lies** (through people) in hopes that the lies will be believed & he won't have to work *as* hard, to trick & spiritually over-power you/us.

Choose...decide adamantly...*today*...that you will <u>no longer</u> sit in the devil's spiritual-stew-pot while he stirs you into a *lesser* form of yourself. ***Awareness is key*** & ***knowledge is power***. If you've come to THIS place, you have both awareness & knowledge...& <u>all</u> excuses are stripped from your mental-victim-*vault*.

God requires <u>all</u> of us to take **ownership** of our spiritual & natural Lives via help from His Word & help from The Holy Spirit. **No longer** choose to believe that "*this is just how things are*" or "*this is just how things have been*" or "*this is all that I've ever known*" or "*this is just the way it is*" or "*this is just what I am used to*". **It is going to take (y)our belief in God's <u>Higher</u> Thought & Purpose that can pull you OUT of the demonic-deception that has spiritually blinded & spiritually numbed you (us) up until now** (Isaiah 55:7-9, 11), making you think that there is no other 'Way'.

Will we choose the <u>Better</u> *Way*...or WILL WE DECIDE TO **STAY** in the *familiarity* of the spiritually-irresponsible?

Now...Ignorance is no longer a 'wild card'.

    Now...we *all* know better.

        Now...it is time for us to

            DO...BETTER...... (*spiritually*).

SUMMARY

...the forsaken one...

he (lower-cased intentionally) is **jealous** & *angry*.

–For he is the *forsaken* one.

he is envious & prideful because of the **ONE** Promise that he has from God...which is *eternal damnation*.

The devil is resentful of man-kind because we have MANY Promises from God!!!!! The Promises that God offers <u>us</u> are good & are not of evil (Jeremiah 29:11).

The devil ***not*** ***have*** the same hopeful out-look, *nor* does he even have a chance... *at reconciliation,* because he is the *forsaken* one. The devil caused *himself* to become forsaken...

...**Even the devil's** power **is subservient to God's Creation called**: *man-kind*. It is God Himself that made this spiritual regulation! It is God Himself Who decided to share **His** Power *with* man-kind; which places the devil unequivocally in subjection *to* **our** Power, which IS God's Word.

The devil's *only* strength is demonic-*influence*, which is called *manipulation*. Manipulation is merely influence *with* improper, secretive, **opportunistic-motives**. *Not all* influence is good.

–The devil will always use spiritually-submitted humans to try to force *his* will on others through *hidden* agendas. *Manipulation* is influence from a **disguised heart**; Manipulation contains *selfish, sneaky, subjective* intentions. One of the greatest lessons my pastor/Life coach Apostle Jacqueline Clark taught me is: " *The only difference between influence &*

manipulation is motive."

The devil's power is 3rd rate. This is why *he has to trick people with lies & empty promises in order to gain compliant followers & ignorant souls.* Why? **Because the devil cannot win people with the Truth**

...

...And the Truth... is that the devil is the *forsaken* one.

The enemy of man (the devil) is *compassion-less*...and *purposely* seeks joy *from* the pain of **others**. –he is the original sadist that humans *foolishly* mimic. Daily, the devil seeks to exploit people in hopes that they will submit *their* higher, **Godly**-Power *to* him; so that through *their* submission (to the devil's subservient power), he can attempt **only**, to use THIS as a tactic to get '*back*'at God. Once again, this is <u>all</u> because of his **now**-position, as the *forsaken one*.

As children, we have no control over our environments. But as adults, we *own* responsibility for our Lives, whether or not we walk in this responsibility. A part of the **God**-Power that Jesus extended to/shares *with* us ...is the **Power of** *Choice*.

As adults, there's no more finger-pointing.
Yes, we can recall what we went through; the whys
& the effects. *These* are called facts...
But what happens **after** the facts? How did **you**
choose a **better** way when taking control over your
own Life?

All of this is being stated to reveal that we now
KNOW (after this knowledge The Holy Spirit shared
with us)...that we have:
* the **Power of Choice** to walk INTO a **TRAP,** or
* the **Power of Choice** to seek God's Will, Heart,
Word to stay OUT of a **TRAP.** –&/or we have
* the **Power of Choice** to work with Yahweh God to
be *released from* a **TRAP...**
　　... (that possibly, we had no idea that we were even in or
that...we **voluntarily** *chose to be a part of).*

The devil himself walked into the 1st **TRAP** that he
created for *himself,* via disobedience unto God.
Through time, the devil has crafted **TRAP**s (for
people) & honed these **TRAP**s into different levels
of *low.* All schemes, plots, plans, ploys, deceptions

from the devil are <u>intended</u> to BIND your spiritual
& natural Life...and make you *believe* that through
your conduct & circumstances...you are now forsak-
en.

But this is a lie!
The *devil*...is the *forsaken* one. God promised US
(not the devil) that He would **never** leave *us* or for-
sake *us*. **It is only** through <u>our decision</u> **to alienate
God, God's Word & God's Will, that we could** *ever*
be separate from God's Intentions.

The devil is trying to reshape/persuade your thinking & *manipulate you* **mentally**... *into* a forsaken
vessel. You can only recreate what you are. –And
this is what the devil aims to do *daily*; get *spiritually, low-level-thinking* humans to submit *their* **God**-
given Power to *him* (through lies & deceit), so that
through the humans' demonic **adherence**, the devil
replicates a *forsaken* mind-set... in the submissive
human.

The 10, *few* ingredients we covered are the *forsaken*
one's tools to lure you away from *your* place as a
(spiritually) KEPT-one.

The devil cannot make us (adults) DO <u>anything</u>!!! he can *only* lie to us, to get us to put OURSELVES in *his* TRAPs, then ...<u>attempt to brainwash us OUT of</u>: **prophetic** (spiritual foresight) / **apostolic** (spiritual authority & proper order) / **GOD-LIKE-**Thinking. The devil does this in hopes that we will stay in these mental, spiritual, physical, emotional, financial & social TRAPs *long* enough, so that **we** will inadvertently take over *his* work & ignorantly reproduce his demonic lies & TRAPs into the lives of those connected to us (a.k.a. being the gateway/conductors of generational & relational curses).

<u>**This is all accomplished through humans believing in the lies of the *forsaken* one.**</u>

Misery loves company.
Doesn't it make sense that the devil would want company in a *forsaken* state?
–Especially company from people who God has Loved, Died & Resurrected ***Himself*** for????
–For a people that God Sacrificed **Himself** to give man-kind a *second* chance at Life & for a renewed relationship *with* God...
...Once God sentenced the devil to an exiled, *forsak-*

en existence, the devil was not offered **any** additional chance at spiritual parole. Nor will he *ever* be...

The *forsaken* one is the ULTIMATE hater.
The devil's philosophy is: "...if you can't beat
'em...TRICK & **TRAP** 'em!" The devil will *always*
seek to make man-kind a positioned pawn in his
sick-spiritual games of destruction, degradation,
duality-deception & despair.

The devil likes to *quench his ego* with *(y)our* tears of
sorrow that are connected to (*y)our*: decided doubt,
displayed disobedience, & divulged disappointment.
The devil *relishes* coaching you/us to become a spiritually, *faithless* vessel, numb & apathetic in Life,
*with no desire to do anything but seek earthly seda-
tives* for spiritual pain & spiritual disconnection.

As long as we are NOT doing things God's Way, the
devil knows that this makes us AUTOMATICALLY
defaulted ...to the *devil's* side. –No matter how much
man-interpreted 'good' ...we '*do*'.

Ignorance is *not* bliss.
This is another lie of the devil. Ignorance can be defined as not knowing knowledge that one *SHOULD*

know. Ignorance is like having on a blind fold that you have the power to take off BEFORE you walk off of the side of a cliff; yet *choosing* to keep it on, while wrongly *believing* that you are a captive. **Wisdom is crying out to all of us!** (Proverbs 1: 20-29) Wisdom is saying that it is time for us to **stop** being spiritually-blind. Our excuses are officially *expired*.

....

Through this prose, The Holy Spirit has taught & reminded us that because of Christ Jesus' Holy Sacrifice of Life for us, we have God's Power extended *to us*. And *with* this GREAT, Spiritual Gift of *Himself* FOR us, God *still* did not remove our God-given **Power of Choice.**

Remember, we have:
* the **Power of Choice** to walk INTO a **TRAP,** or
* the **Power of Choice** to seek God's Will, Heart, & His Word to stay OUT of a **TRAP** –&/or we have
* the **Power of Choice** to work with Yahweh God to be *released from* a **TRAP...**
   ...(that possibly, we had no idea that we were even in or that
         *we **voluntarily** chose to be a part of).*

The devil's options are up. *The devil is* the *forsaken* one. he does not have the **Power of Choice**. The devil is **condemned** to: his original, contaminated thinking, the eternal *fallen*-sentence that his spiritual lifestyle produced, as well as, the spiritual execution that awaits him. *Fury* is his incentive to gain more (human) followers.

You & I have traveled somewhat of a rough road before getting to THIS place...We've consciously & unconsciously made good & bad decisions in Life *up until now*. We played victim whenever it 'tasted' good. But with all that we've learned up to THIS moment –up to reading *this* sentence, we **know** that all things, actions & thoughts outside of God's Will & God's Word is vanity. It's futile. It's hopeless.

When vain imaginations try to cloud our minds with negative thoughts that are contrary to what God says, *let us cast those thoughts down* (2 Corinthians 10:5)! If it is not a thought or an action or a plan or an idea that can be attributed to God's Nature, then it is a thought or an action or a plan or an idea that can be **defaulted** & considered a *casted* lure... it is a thought or an action or a plan or an idea TO a **TRAP**... for you/us... from... the *forsaken* one.

Let us rise UP & <u>GROW</u>:

*in Faith in God,

*in Hope in God,

* **in** (heart) **Knowledge of God's Word** &

*in Love *in* God.

<u>Let us pray for **new** hearts of flesh</u> to RE-
PLACE...our *old* hearts of stone & spiritual stub-
bornness that we robed *with* rusty rebellion; –let us
pray for new hearts that *long* after Father God's
Truth & *detest* man's religiousness. Let us begin *or*
continue to Trust & Seek & Ask that The Holy
Spirit will continue to be our Guide & *Mighty*, Wise
Counselor & definite, <u>Best</u> Friend. Let us seek *daily*
to be more submitted to Yahweh God than *yesterday*.

··

If you/we use the **Power of Choice** & opt to <u>not</u> do
these things, this *decision of refusal* proves that you/we
CHOOSE... to lay (y)our **God**-given Power at the
feet of the *subservient, forsaken* one (whether, due to:
pleasure, doubt, fear, or pain)...
...**and with the blind-fold NOW removed...**
CHOOSING to say "*no*" to God's Way...

... you choose to **WILLINGLY** lie down...

...& *spiritually*...become the picture on
the front book-cover.

ABOUT THE AUTHOR

(Photo by: *S. Wright Photography* ©)

Andy Cooper is an author of non-fiction content & poetry. She is a robust, independent-thinker who has overcome great adversities.

Andy Cooper has personal experience in relation to: family apprehensions, mental health issues, personality concerns, anxiety, drug & alcohol use/ abuse, low-self-esteem, fear, doubt, hopelessness, insomnia, weight-loss & weight-gain, apathy, teen pregnancy, adoption, depression, physical / verbal / mental / emotional / financial / spiritual- abuse, 'hater'-attacks (direct & indirect), suppression, oppression, regression, worry & personal crisis (to name a few)...all the while, operating in demanding positions with incessant, high-stress levels, professionally & personally.

YET, Divinely...Andy has overcome time & time again, with Wisdom & Emotional Intelligence as her collective rewards. Andy Cooper desires to share her Life's lessons with individuals who want to become wiser & stronger in their _own_ lives, **no** matter the trials one may face.

Andy Cooper loves Travel, Peace & Wisdom.

Made in the USA
Columbia, SC
04 February 2018